Woman U

The Highly Sensitive Woman's Guide to Radiant Energy and Unstoppable Confidence, Including a 21-Day Plan to Kick Sugar's Hold on You

Woman Unleashed

The Highly Sensitive Woman's Guide to Radiant Energy and Unstoppable Confidence, Including a 21-Day Plan to Kick Sugar's Hold on You

By Jenn Edden, CHHC

ISBN: 978-0-9884471-5-8

YouSpeakIt
PUBLISHING
The Easy Way
to Get Your Book
Done Right ™

www.YouSpeakItPublishing.com

Dedication

Dedicated to the spirited, spunky, insightful, kindhearted, funny, generous, one-of-a-kind, God-broke-the-mold-when-He-made-you highly sensitive woman. You, my friend, were the inspiration for writing this book and for sure, you make the world go 'round.

Acknowledgments

Where to begin? So many people have helped bring this book to life through their wisdom, guidance, and ability to let their light shine.

My rock, my love, my biggest cheerleader for seeing me for who I was before I got here: Joe Edden.

My soul brother and musician extraordinaire for always putting me back on my path: Youssif Eid.

My forever-mentor and teacher for awakening me to the work of coaching: Joshua Rosenthal.

My kids: Luke, Caitlin, and Sydney, for expanding my heart and teaching me about living in the moment.

My uncle, Pete, for teaching me that commitment, hard work, and perseverance pays off.

My cousin, David, for being a bright light of all that is possible when you live your passion.

My mother-in-law, Joanne Edden, for showing me that age is just a number.

My grandmother, Concetta, for teaching me that life has only the limits you put on it.

My friend Robert Notter, for being the reminder that your past does not define you.

My parents, for showing me that forgiveness is the only way to live.

Maura and Keith Leon, for the constant reminder to trust the process.

LiYana Silver, my first relationship mentor, for expanding my consciousness about what is possible when you let go.

My clients. Every one of you. You know who you are. Thank you for allowing me to be a part of your world as you grow and expand and light the world with your brilliance.

Contents

CHAPTER FIVE

Introduction

I'm about to teach you some simple yet profound processes that will help you free up the energy in your body and mind. They will naturally allow your gifts to reveal themselves to you and to the world.

This book is about understanding and working with:

- The gifts that God gave you when you were born
- All the talents and natural abilities that get buried and go unnoticed
- All the emotions that get trapped
- All the crap you've grown up with
- Everything that has contributed to those gifts being buried

Highly sensitive women are quick to absorb everything around them. When you are highly sensitive, it's easy to believe what's being said to you, whether it's negative or positive. This is especially true when you are growing up.

Often you're not aware of your gifts or you haven't allowed them to evolve or grow. It's even hard to know what they are or who you are. As you get clear, you start to really appreciate yourself. In their own time, these challenges and confusing thoughts reveal themselves.

You can take certain steps to help them come forward:

- Clear out
- Clean up
- Simplify
- Take time for gratitude

Life takes on all-new meaning. Life actually becomes really fun.

You are no longer in a place of:

- Overwhelm
- Rushing
- Needing to get stuff done to check it off a list to feel worthy and good about yourself

You get to ask yourself:

What can I do with my life now?

What can I bring to the world?

How good am I?

How good can I really become in my life, given what gifts God has given me?

You no longer wake up just making it through the day, thinking about who does or doesn't like you, being defined by that number on a scale, or perhaps when that next raise or promotion is coming. All of that just seems to drift away.

I wrote this book because I'm a very visual person, and I personally enjoy seeing concepts on paper. I know that a lot of people around me — especially clients who work with me — enjoy that physical copy as well. While it's great to be spoken to, and to be inspired by hearing people speak and whatnot, having a written copy is priceless. You can write notes and jot things down in a book.

I also wrote the book because after many years of coaching, I knew it was time to take what I've learned through trial and error and bring it to the masses. Some of you may not be ready for one-on-one work, or you might not even have known that I existed — because I'm one person in the sea of billions. But now I can reach you through this book. Now is the opportunity for me to teach hundreds, thousands, millions of people what I've learned. I can help not only my family and myself, but all of my clients and people who work with me, to maximize our potential in a way that's simple, effective, and allows us to feel empowered.

If you're anything like me, the best way to use this book is to pick a chapter and just read it.

I'd be lying if I said, "You must read it in sequential order."

Go ahead and be your fabulous self and read it the way you want to — I know you are a rebel anyway. Go ahead and just open it up, find a chapter that resonates most with you, and enjoy it. When you're done with that, and you've taken the time to do the fun action items that I give in each section — please don't rush those — then go onto the next chapter.

But really, you can't get this wrong. You get to pick the order in which you want to learn and grow and read. Keep it simple.

If there's a concept or something that you either feel confused about or overwhelmed by, lean into it. Don't just blow past it and move onto the next chapter. I learn a lot about myself by reading about concepts that I don't quite get at first. I just keep rereading and asking others for help in understanding it. Usually it's the lesson in the whole book that I most need to get.

Sometimes confusion is a block to what we really need to learn most.

What not to do:

- Do not — *do not* — let your confusion about a concept, an experience I share, or an Action item stop you.
- Do not let it convince you to move on or away from it.
- Do not let it make you tell yourself one of those negative things.

You don't get to do that in this book! You get to totally handle it as it comes, and ask for some help. Feeling confused and getting help is a good lesson, so that's how I want you to read this book.

I hope that reading this book helps you to gain:

- **Insight** into who you were when you were born
- **Inspiration** to do the work on this planet that you were meant to do
- **A deep self-love and appreciation** for who you are
- **Bravery and courage** to get out there
- **The knowledge** that if I can do this, you can do this
- **Freedom** from whatever—up until now—you've told yourself that has been holding you back from being your best self (they're all lies anyway!)
- **Clarity** to make decisions, not second-guess yourself

I am no different from you; I just stepped up.

The opportunity presented itself, and I said, "Yes."

When you say yes, you start to see life as an adventure, and not something to fear and just wait for the next day to come, but as a gift. Every day.

My favorite line is, "What's the biggest gift someone could give you? The present."

The present moment, right here, now. Not yesterday, not tomorrow, right here and now.

And for those of you who are skipping through the book, be sure to check out my Next Steps chapter.

In it I offer my thoughts on how to make all your work permanent, including a very special gift just for purchasing my book. You can access your gift by heading over to www.womanunleashedgift.com.

CHAPTER
ONE

Know Thyself,
Know Thy Worth

WHO ARE YOU?

It takes courage…to endure the sharp pains of self discovery rather than choose to take the dull pain of unconsciousness that would last the rest of our lives.
~ Marianne Williamson
A Return to Love: Reflections on the Principles
of "A Course in Miracles"

In all the years that I have been coaching women, I have found that until you truly know who you are and how in your sensitivity you differ from others, you can never really understand other people and understand the world.

So I always like to start with what I call the foundation work: know yourself. Then you're pretty much able to figure out everything else in life.

Highly Sensitive Women and the Rest of the World

There are different types of people out there. Not bad or good, right or wrong, but there's this particular kind of woman—myself included—who has a different view of the world. I'm a highly sensitive woman living in a not-so-highly-sensitive world.

As a highly sensitive woman, when you were growing up you might have heard:

- You're a crybaby.
- You're overly emotional.
- You take things too seriously.
- Why can't you let it roll off your back?

When you're a highly sensitive woman, you can scan a room and sense the feelings of the people. You have a pulse on energy as it moves or doesn't move in a conversation. As a highly sensitive woman, at a party you might feel like you're the odd one out.

You're always the one asking yourself:

What's wrong with me?

Is it just me?

Why don't I fit in?

Why can't I just let it roll off my back?

When you don't yet understand that you're sensitive, you may behave in ways that limit yourself:

- Second-guessing yourself
- Over-feeling or over-thinking things
- Being mindful always of how somebody else will feel
- Feeling easily insulted or getting hurt feelings
- Having a hard time letting go of past hurt or anger

But when you realize and appreciate that sensitivity is a special gift of yours, you can feel more confident about yourself. You begin to understand that you are just that in-tune that you pick up on subtle or not-so-subtle energy changes in the world. And that's okay.

How Were You Raised?

This is really important.

Whether or not you discover you're highly sensitive really affects how you view your childhood. It affects the beliefs you've made up about yourself.

Highly sensitive women — including myself — see the world very differently as they grow up:

- Change is difficult and can easily bring on feelings of anxiousness.

- Feeling so much without understanding it can definitely cause anxiety and nervousness.

- School is filled with all sorts of highs and deep lows.

- You may be ostracized or ridiculed by less-sensitive people, even your parents, if they are not aware of their own sensitivity and therefore don't know how to handle yours appropriately.

- Because of your difference, you may feel like something is broken inside, or that you have a weakness, or that you need to be fixed.

Maybe you cried a lot. I did. That was how I processed feelings and let stuff go.

Unless you can heal that from the past, you're not able to feel your most empowered self. Something is always missing. You need to know that you were perfectly fine growing up. You were just highly sensitive living in an insensitive world without the tools to navigate the ups and downs in a way that took care of you.

As soon as I help women identify that there wasn't ever anything wrong with them — that actually, they just have the gift (not curse) of sensitivity — they're able to fully come into themselves. They can let all that baggage go, the baggage of not fitting in and feeling anxious as a kid, feeling *over*sensitive, as if that's a negative.

When you are a highly sensitive child, and you have all those "feelers" out in the world, your childhood doesn't really look like everyone else's. This is why how you were raised can make a big difference in how you view the world and yourself as an adult.

As an example, I'll share with you that as a kid, I sweated a lot. Nobody could understand why I couldn't stop sweating. I also had TMJ (temporomandibular joint disorder), and no one understood why. Doctors, even the dentist, didn't know why my jaw locked out of nowhere and then I couldn't talk until the muscles relaxed. If someone had identified that we just moved to a new town and a new high school and that adjusting to change didn't come easily for me, then a locked jaw would have made sense.

Highly sensitive women internalize when there's no safe way or space in which to release feelings. So while you think this is really you, it's not. It's just you out of balance, and frankly not having a safe enough space to share with people who understand you.

Fast-forward to adulthood, and you think that's who you are; you have all these issues and you wonder what's wrong with you. The truth is, when you were growing up, you just didn't know who you were. If you have a dominant father or mother, and they don't know that you're this way and they don't have these traits, then you tend to clam up and be quiet, and internalize more.

When we internalize, a lot of us highly sensitive women have anxiety and turn to food for comfort.

It's always a good idea to start by taking a good look at how you were raised.

What Are Your Beliefs?

I always address beliefs with my clients. I relate this to living your fullest potential.

To live a life unleashed, you need to know some basic information about yourself:

- Who you are
- How you were raised
- What you believe
- What as a child you saw as being normal and adopted subconsciously as your own beliefs

I find a lot of people feel stuck in their lives because they took on beliefs that do not serve them, but they are unaware that those beliefs are running their every move.

As an example, let's say a client I work with believes that because she grew up shy. Well, then, she must just be shy and she will always be that way. Therefore, asking for what she wants and speaking up for herself when she's feeling put down feels near impossible.

I would guide her to take a look at her childhood and see how she was raised. Maybe she felt shy because being shy was how she felt safe. It's not necessarily true that she's shy because that's always the way she was. It may be because of something like when she was raised, being quiet and shy is what kept her out of harm's way with one or both of her parents. I came to learn that she had a very abusive father, so staying quiet helped her stay safe. This is actually a common scenario.

How do you show up now in the world?

Is that really you, or is that just a belief that you took on from growing up?

You may grow up and take on the beliefs of your parents and think that they're yours. One I see a lot is *mommy guilt*, especially with my mom-entrepreneur clients.

The moms reading this may think: *Oh, I just feel guilty because I'm just wired that way.*

Take a look at your beliefs growing up.

What did your mom believe?

Did your mom believe that she should sacrifice herself every single day and run herself into the ground?

In my case, my mom, and her mom, and her mom all had nervous breakdowns. It has been passed on.

I thought: *Well, the buck stops here. Their belief was that they had to run themselves into the ground to be a good mother and a wife.*

They overdid it, and they were probably highly sensitive — the way I am — and they didn't know their limits.

***Then I grew up and I had to really rewire and rethink:
What are my beliefs around being a mom, and running
a business, and this whole mommy guilt concept?***

I had to realize that it wasn't my belief; it was my
mother's belief that you really have to sacrifice yourself.

Unless you take a look at your beliefs and where they've
come from, you might think that things just are the way
they are. But the truth is that if you know where the
beliefs came from and you really don't identify with
them, you can make really big changes in your life.

That's why it's so important to start with, "Know
Thyself, Know Thy Worth."

Your beliefs rule you, whether you know it or not.
Using my mommy guilt as an example, when I started
changing my belief, I totally broke the family legacy of
nervous breakdowns. I recognized where the feelings
of mommy guilt came from, and I started changing my
belief. I continue to make sure to take care of myself.

My belief now is that a great mother is one who puts
herself first and her family always. By bringing my best
self to my kids, I've now totally changed my future (and
that of my daughters who are watching me). Taking
care of myself might look like getting a sitter during the
week so I can go play tennis, or go work out, or meet a
friend for a cup of tea. I've put aside mommy guilt, not
because of willpower but because I've changed a deep,
limiting belief that I grew up with.

Even though you may be highly sensitive, you don't have to be quiet. Not all highly sensitive women are quiet, such as myself. If you can identify with some of the traits listed here, then you can start taking a look.

Are you more passive in your life?

Are you more like me: assertive but still sensitive to other people's needs?

Sometimes highly sensitive women who are out of balance can actually be aggressive as a way to protect themselves.

Assertive highly sensitive women have their own challenges, as one would imagine. You may be assertive and feel like you're doing the right thing, but you also sense that people around you are uncomfortable (which, side note: it's never really about you).

If you're *passive* and highly sensitive, your needs might not be fulfilled and you can feel that, but don't yet have the tools to speak up. You know that you want to speak up, because you're that in touch with yourself.

Or, if you're *aggressive* and highly sensitive, maybe you're going to bed at night and you're not happy with that aggressiveness. You're so sensitive that you know something's out of balance. At least then you know that it's a protective mechanism, and you can change it, instead of thinking that's just the way you are.

Action Item

Take a minute now and jot down one limiting belief you have and how you will overcome it. Use my mommy guilt example above to help you.

This section is about how to stop, look around, notice, and really understand not only who you are, but also how you became who you are.

NAME YOUR STRENGTHS

Know who you are and be proud of who you are! Identify the things you're naturally good at. While I'm not a pessimist, I truly feel like we live in a negative world of tearing down; just watch the news. Unless you are your own best advocate and rah-rah cheerleader, it's not as easy to get to your really good-feeling place (which I'll describe more later) and to unleash yourself.

For highly sensitive women like me, it's tricky because we're humble. At the same time, if we don't toot our own horns, no one else is going to do it. It's really important that this gets addressed now.

It's okay to own your strengths.

Focus on What's Working and Hire Others for What Isn't

The brain tends to go to what's *not* working. There's a lot of support for this coming from the negative bias of the news or from how we were raised. It's easy to focus on the negative things that happen in a day: we got cut off on the drive home or the kids were screaming all day. It seems far more unusual that when someone asks how your day went that you'll reply with what went well.

It's really important to notice that that's where the brain goes, and to counter that with building a muscle.

You're building a muscle around what *is* working, noticing what *are* your strengths.

My husband, Joe, is super creative, and he's not quite so organized. Super creative, super businessman, but the organizational piece is just not in him, whereas that's my strength. Once he and I had let that go, Joe was able to hire people to help him keep organized. Then his life, confidence, and business took off.

I believe everything is energy. When Joe stopped putting energy into stuff that was difficult and not working, he was able to put all his energy into what he's really good at and what *is* working.

When you focus on what's going right, you're able to let the rest go. I joke around about hiring out because I work with women who don't like to cook and don't know how to cook. They're looking to run their businesses. They invest so much of their energy into what's not working, which is the cooking. My advice is to order from one of those healthy home-delivery meal-in-a-box places, like Blue Apron, or hire someone to help them cook and organize that piece. Then they can put all their energy into things that they enjoy doing.

Like I always tell my clients, "Good feelings build on good feelings."

If you're feeling really good about getting out and networking (if you're an entrepreneur), or if you're a really creative mom who is good at arts and crafts with your kids, then that's the stuff I want you to focus on. Confidence builds on confidence.

If you're spending all day with thoughts like: *I'm not organized, and I'm not creative enough,* you'll get stuck in that.

Like attracts like. Free up your energy so you can naturally bring to yourself what's next in the most joyful way possible.

What You Enjoy Comes Easily and Doesn't Feel Like Work

Most people believe that life is supposed to be difficult and pleasure is something out there to have on vacation. Usually this idea comes from childhood.

Maybe a parent has told us that life is difficult, so we think: *Life must be difficult. I'll save up my fun for vacations and just muscle through my work week.*

People also tend to diminish their strengths. Lots of the women I talk with nonchalantly mention things that they're good at, but they really focus on what they feel they're not at all good at. They tend to depreciate, not celebrate, aspects of themselves that really make them shine.

So when I can get women to figure out what their strengths are — maybe it's forming relationships — they get happy. When you're happy, you bring into your life more of what you want. You no longer experience a constant up-and-down in life in which one day you have a good day, one day you don't have a good day. When you focus on your strengths and use them often, you really stay in the flow (and I'll talk more about that in a later chapter). Life starts to hum and feel good.

Make a List of Your Strengths

We read all these great books and we get really excited.

But then we get really busy:

- The phone is ringing.
- The client is calling.
- The kids are yelling.

Then we don't take any action. I am all about action in this book.

Action Item

Take a look at yourself now.

- Set a timer: ten minutes, because that might be all you can handle (it's all I can handle).
- Write down all the stuff that you're great at.

You'll know what you're really good at, and what your strengths are, because they come so easily to you! In my case, I sometimes can't believe that people pay me to learn how to have my high energy and positive outlook on life.

Another way you'll know your strengths is that you are your happiest; you're elated time flies, and you don't even know that half a day has gone by.

As an example, one of my strengths is that I'm a really good listener. I couldn't believe when I first started coaching that people would pay me to listen and to create a safe space for them to share things that, pretty much, their own mothers didn't know.

I would be in shock that they would say, "I just trust you. There's something about you that's so authentic. I know you're not blowing smoke up my ass, and you're authentic and I trust you, and therefore I want to share with you."

I remember going to my coach, saying, "I can't believe people pay me for this! This is nuts."

I had found one of my core strengths — something that was not only going to help grow my business, but help hundreds of thousands of women have a safe space to share and feel understood. When we provide women safety and understanding, we move mountains.

In a world where confidence doesn't seem to come naturally and easily, especially to highly sensitive women, it is in your best interest to identify who you are and what your specific strengths are. They may not be money-makers for you, but you can do them every single day so that they help you feel good and help build your confidence for those less-than-confident days.

Naming your strengths and remembering them, so they're on the tip of your tongue, will help you:

- Generate radiant energy
- Embody unshakable confidence
- Reach your highest potential

ACT AS IF

You may often take your reality to be your truth, an extrapolation of where you're going to be in five years, when it couldn't be further from the truth!

The only reason that I'm living the reality that I'm living right now is because I think, feel, and believe that this is how it has to be; this is how it is.

The only way to get to the next place you want to get to in life is to think past where you are—and start acting *as if*. It's not about pretending; I want to be very clear about that.

Acting as if includes many aspects:

- Acting
- Feeling
- Seeing
- Thinking
- Visualizing

Say, for instance, that you want to be a coach or consultant for large groups of people. See yourself onstage with tens of thousands of people listening and getting inspired. It may feel uncomfortable at first, but if you think it long enough, it will start to feel good.

If you feel unsuccessful, and you think that thought all day long, it's just the reverse. When you focus on the client you didn't get, or that job that fell through, you just keep manifesting the negative.

Instead, visualize getting what you want. Act, feel, see, and think of what that will be like. Visualize it happening right now.

Action Item

Create a vision board. I love them and find them to be extremely helpful in visualizing.

- Pull out your favorite magazines.
- Cut out all pictures that call out to you and make you smile.
- Make a collage by arranging and pasting the pictures on oak tag board. (Remember oak tag?)

My vision board sits in my office, framed. A few of my visions it depicts are visiting Ireland, making my own snow days, and helping others have a future.

Feel Your Way to Your Future

T. Harv Eker is the author of *The Millionaire Mind* and a host of seminars and programs that help people clear money issues and take control of their lives. Years ago, he was a life-changer for my husband and me around our finances. He has taught that in order to make changes, you really need to feel different.

I'll never forget what he said: "If you want to make that big income, and you want to live an extraordinary life, you need to do the things that bring that feeling to you."

Eker said to go out to the most expensive restaurant in town, even if you have to save up for an entire month to be able to do it guilt-free, because you budgeted that money toward it. It will change your life, because you will feel what it feels like to have disposable income.

Joe and I had really been struggling. We actually started doing that exercise, saving up for a month and then spending it. We could feel what it would be like if we weren't struggling and we had some disposable income. Now it has translated into reality. But it started with a feeling.

If you've already identified yourself as a highly sensitive woman, this part will be kind of easy for you, because you feel a lot as a matter of course. Your ability to feel is a powerful tool, but it may have been keeping you stuck. If you aren't aware of it and how it works, your focus on negative things may have kept you from moving forward.

Now I am asking you to feel your way into the future for what you *want*, not feel around for why you're not getting what you want: why so-and-so wasn't nice that day or why your feelings got hurt.

Instead, I want you to focus on:

- The positive
- What you want
- Using your feelings to get you to the next place

I have a dear friend who's a musician, and I always tell him, "Go find an empty stage, get on it, and just stare out and visualize the crowd of people you want to be playing in front of."

Experience it before it happens; that way you can bring the experience to you. That's what I mean by feel your way to the future. Go do things that bring it to you.

Look the Part

I love my family and respect them, especially my mom. But when I was growing up, my mom wasn't exactly the epitome of sexy. She was modest. But I felt sexy and wanted to express that. On the outside, I wore a lot of hiking boots and sandals, shorts, and T-shirts, but inside, I felt sexy.

One day I said to myself: *I'm going to go out and get my outside to match my inside.*

I started buying more fitted clothing. I started buying things that were a little shorter, that showed off my figure more. The truth is that it was uncomfortable.

So let me just note this about highly sensitive women: *Change is not comfortable.*

But change is needed if we're going to reach our highest potential, live unleashed, and be our best version of ourselves out in the world. If you've chosen to read this, that is what you want too, so you've got to take my word on this: change is not comfortable.

With highly sensitive women, myself included, I tend to feel comfortable wearing the same old clothes I've been wearing for years. I believe clothes have energy, and there's a level of comfort wearing the same stuff. But there is some cool energy that comes with buying new clothes. I'm not saying just go ahead and go out and buy a whole new wardrobe, but what I mean is, go ahead and try buying something new.

How does it feel?

I want to know. Email me and tell me.

There's something energetic and exciting about putting on fresh and new. If you want that high-profile job, or you want to be that mom who does look and feel sexy, and if you're like me and feel a little risqué, then go ahead and buy those earrings or something for yourself that helps you to play the part.

When you act as if, over time it starts to feel normal. At this point in time for me, *not* looking sexy and wearing oversized stuff feels awkward. Actually I started getting rid of everything that was not me and donated it. I'll discuss more about this kind of clearing out in a later chapter.

When I look in the closet now, I see how I've grown into the new version of me. It's all from acting as if; knowing that I wanted to be something else, but I wasn't quite there yet. Then eventually I got there. I highly recommend you do the same.

Take a minute now and think about either what you aspire to, or something that scares you, something that makes you say, "Oh, that's not me!"

Let me tell you, I said that for years. Now, I look at myself, and my face has changed. I look different. It's amazing how that works!

If you're looking to change and reach your highest potential and unleash yourself, remember that change is good; change is necessary.

Ask Yourself Empowering Questions

When people are looking to make changes, they'll talk and talk about it. For instance, people with food cravings may try to talk themselves out of it. The mind runs in circles if you talk to it. But if you ask it a question, it interrupts what I call the *mental masturbation*. It interrupts the mental masturbation altogether and it pushes you to have a different perspective.

For those readers who have kids, you all know that when your kids are having a tantrum, if you ask them, "Did the Easter Bunny, or Santa Claus, or a pink elephant just run across the lawn? Did you see it?"

The kids will stop and say, "What? I missed it!"

And they will totally forget about what just upset them. It's because we've interrupted their tantrum with a question. When you're feeling in that stuck place, go ahead and stop your tantrum and ask yourself a question. Not just any question, because we all know that asking yourself if you just saw the pink elephant will do you no good. Ask yourself an empowering question.

I'll give you an example:

What would a successful, physically fit, confident woman do in this situation?

Imagine you're dealing with nighttime cravings, standing in front of the open cupboard — go there with me now.

Maybe you're saying to yourself: *Ah, but I just want those chips tonight! I want them! I just have to have them!* even though you know how they make you feel the next day.

Ask yourself:

If I were a physically fit, confident, secure, woman who loves myself, what would I do right now?

You might rethink:

Well, I'll go have a cup of tea, or go for a walk, or do something that would make me feel good, because that's what that type of a woman would do.

I used to be that woman in front of the open cupboard. Now I just don't do that stuff anymore. This is a newer version of me. It's not that I do it from a place of willpower or deprivation, it's because of the many years in which I acted as if. I became that confident, fit, successful woman. You ask yourself that question, and see what comes up. I invite you to do it right now.

If you're on a job interview or there's something going on where you're not feeling so secure, go ahead and ask yourself what that confident woman would do. You'll be surprised by the answers. All of a sudden, your brain will come up with new answers because you asked it a new question.

I know those who are similar to me who may be concerned that acting as if is just pretending. You do not want to pretend or to be phony because that doesn't work either. But I assure you, you can find a way to act authentically and show up in the world, even if it's just when you're at home in a safe place. You don't even have to be out in the world to test-drive this.

I promise you, if you repeat this over time, it will feel natural. That's what we're looking for here: We're looking for you to be your authentic self, for you to do it in a way that feels right, and then over time, you become it.

LAURA'S TESTIMONIAL

Simply put, Jenn is the bomb. I've been working with her for four years, and I honestly cannot imagine a future without her. I was a completely different, less outspoken, less confident twenty-eight-year-old version of myself back then. I initially hired her to help start my health coaching business, but as time passed, I changed and so did my career.

I am now a Pilates teacher and teacher trainer at one of the top studios in Manhattan, and I love every second. I had always lived by other people's rules instead of making my own, and that is exactly what Jenn has helped me discover and create. She continues to support and empower me to unapologetically express myself, and to be selective of whom and what I choose to give energy to. She challenges me to chase opportunities that make me uncomfortable. I am forever grateful for her being a part of my life and growth as a human. I am unstoppable.

~ Laura Constantiner
Baller Pilates Instructor & CHHC
www.dailydubie.com

CHAPTER
TWO

Keep it Simple

YOUR SCHEDULE

Life is really simple,
but we insist on making it complicated.

~ Confucius

Your schedule is how you spend your time. For highly sensitive women, it can be difficult to say no to others. We have a tendency toward people pleasing. If you don't address your schedule, you can lose a lot of time doing for others. You can get scattered and lose track of your goals, creations, and dreams.

You say yes to everyone else:

- Your kids
- Your clients
- Your spouse
- Your coworkers

When there's something for others, like getting the kids to school, or meeting with a client, my guess is it's cemented in your brain. I know my client calls are all written down in the schedule.

Then you get frustrated trying to do stuff for yourself; you get frustrated and want to give up.

If It's Not Written Down, It Ain't Happening

Maybe you're a mom and you start taking that new exercise class in town or better yet, you've been wanting to start your own business. Maybe you're an entrepreneur with a great new business idea and you're getting psyched or it's the new year and you're feeling motivated to get in the best shape of your life. I've had many a moment with that thought! And then — BOOM!

What happens?

It's not written down.

There is something really special and important and grounding in writing your schedule down; it grounds you when you can see your plan. It also gives you the opportunity to move it around in your schedule. But you can't move it if it's not written down.

When I started writing down what most people might think is silly: "Jenn works out 9–10 a.m.," it became real.

It was on the schedule.

Clients and friends ask me, "How do you get so much done in a day while raising three small kids? Then you work out in the morning, then you run the business, and now you're writing a book, and your husband looks pretty dang happy, and you cook most of your meals. How do you do it?"

I tell them, "One of my gifts is organization. My schedule is what I consider a living, breathing organism."

The schedule is something that ebbs and flows; it's not something that you write and when it doesn't work, you get disappointed. Your schedule is like a draft of your life.

Just write it down, and just know it's a draft, which means it gets revised every day. You can't be attached to it not being revised. That's why some people don't want to write items down, because they don't want to feel bad that they didn't get them all done.

I write all my tasks and events down—or I use the task management feature in my email software—and then when they don't get done, I just move them to another day, and then at least they're always in my consciousness.

There's nothing wrong with you wanting to be there for others. But controlling your schedule is your lifeline to getting to where you want to go.

Give Your Schedule Room to Breathe

If you're a type-A person like me who likes to jam everything into a day, you get overexcited in the morning. Sometimes people are fearful that they're never going to get it all done, so they pack their day full of everything they can think of.

You sit down with your cup of coffee and breakfast and tell yourself: *Okay, I'm going to put something in at 9:00, 9:15, 10:00, 11:00, and I'll skip lunch so I can fit in this other thing at noon...*

Not only can you not even *physically* get it all done, but you also don't feel successful about all the things you have done. Jamming too many things in a schedule actually negates all the positive things you did that day. You probably know as well as I do that when you start negating all the positives, they start to outweigh how good you feel about yourself. They become more prominent in your mind than the positive things you've done.

I'm all about feeling good. I really want you to feel good at the end of your day. You can only really do that if you don't keep jamming extra stuff into your schedule that, deep down, you know is unrealistic and won't get done. When you can limit that behavior, you will find that you actually start to enjoy and take comfort in having a schedule.

When I look at my schedule now, I just smile and breathe easily, because I know the stuff there is manageable and it's going to get done. When you allow this space in your schedule and accept that things will change and that they can be moved around, you view your schedule with excitement, not stress.

Yes, it's important to have a schedule, but it's got to be one that makes you feel good.

Put Aside How You Feel and Just Do It

When you feel good, you get attached to feeling good. You want to do more of whatever it is that makes you feel good. But with a schedule, you actually have to *do* what's on the schedule. It's the piece about scheduling that always makes me chuckle, because it's like the little asterisk — you actually have to *do* what's on the schedule.

Remember:

- Write stuff down.
- Don't be attached to getting it all done.
- Know that it's breathable.
- Know that it's changeable.
- There's no such thing as a perfect schedule.

The thing is, you can't make the schedule and then say: *Oh, I really don't feel like a 10:00 appointment* or *I don't feel like working out this morning.*

You don't have to do what's on the schedule forever, and force square pegs into round holes. But you need to work your schedule long enough to understand whether it works.

Then go ahead and assess:

- What did you like about it?

- What really didn't work?
- How does it feel?

You can't do that by just looking at it on a piece of paper. You actually have to live the schedule for a week or two. In this stage, you have to put aside your resistance.

Put aside your feelings of "I don't want to do it," or "It feels hard," and just see how it goes.

Imagine you're starting a new early-morning workout routine. You feel really excited by it in the beginning.

Then, thoughts creep in: *Hmm, I'm not so sure if I want to keep doing this.*

But if you just put those thoughts to the side and keep checking in with yourself, you can get to a point where it feels good. You'll feel really good that you stuck with it. It becomes part of the scheduled routine and it just gets done.

That's why you need to put aside feelings in the beginning and just work the schedule.

If you don't work the schedule, and you just look at it on a piece of paper, you will never actually know if it works for you. If you want to unleash yourself and reach your full potential, your schedule really is what's going to get you there, because it's how you spend your time.

- Take a hard look at how you spend your time.
- Write stuff down.
- Don't be overly hard on yourself.
- Give yourself a schedule where you're able to win at the end of the day.
- Work the schedule to assess whether what you've written down is working.

Action Item

- Set a timer for ten minutes.
- Schedule your week—write it all down.
- Just do it. Put in everything you currently do on automatic and things that you've been wanting to do.

The day I wrote down that I "pay bills on Tuesdays" was the year that I paid my bills every Tuesday and never, I mean never missed a payment. It was scheduled!

A little note to you, since I've been doing this for so many years: The first time you write something down, you're probably not going to get it right.

I've revised, and re-revised my schedule until it's just right, and then the summer comes with the kids out of school and it all goes to hell! Then I re-revise it; then come the fall, I revise again. So if you have kids, leave lots of breathing room through the summer or holidays, and then bring it back in the fall.

As the seasons ebb and flow, especially for us sensitive types, so do our moods and so do our schedules. In the winter, it's really important to make more time for rest. Find a way to do it even if you feel like you can't. I actually put rest in my schedule, because it's the time of the year when most mammals hibernate. They slow down.

Otherwise, you can get run down and be more likely to get sick with the flu, colds, and sinus stuff. I tend to not get that, and neither does my family. It's because I ebb and flow with the seasons. Make sure that you're aware of that.

While you're building what I call the *new model of not overdoing it*, you need to start saying no to people and events that don't fit your schedule or don't fit your agenda. You can just breathe, stay present, and not let yourself get overwhelmed. Know that it's just a muscle you're building, and that it just takes time, and that it is possible.

Start with one thing that you would like to remove or reduce.

If you're not sure what that one would be, try asking yourself:

If I only had a year to live, would I want to go to that event, see that individual, do that thing that I have written in my schedule?

If that's too far out, hell, ask:

If I only had a month to live...

Then you watch and see how you tighten up your schedule. The truth really comes out when you give yourself the exercise of only having a month, three months, or a year to live.

STAYING PRESENT

As a highly sensitive woman, you can quickly go from feeling calm and secure and grounded to feeling pulled off your center. Someone gives you a call, or something goes wrong with the spouse, or something with a client didn't go quite right. It happens to all of us, but if you can find a way — your own way — to re-ground, and come back to center, it will really help keep you productive through the emotionally difficult times.

Focus on the Task at Hand

Anxiety is something that can come up very quickly. All of a sudden, you don't feel productive and you don't know what to do. If you scheduled a meeting for Monday at 10:00 a.m., then that's all you need to think about for that allotted time. Just focus on that one thing.

If you stay present, you actually can't be worried. It is the coolest thing I've ever experienced. Worrying comes from thinking about the future or the past. But if you're actually in the present moment, you can't worry.

Action Item

1. Set a timer for two minutes, one minute, or maybe thirty seconds is enough for you.

2. Think about what's going on right now:

   - Are you're hungry or thirsty?
   - Are you tired?
   - Do you feel rushed today?
   - Do you need to stop and take a quick break?

When you are engaged in one task but thinking about another, that's when anxiety and worry and all this waste of mental energy comes in.

You can't be anxious if you're driving, because that's all your doing: driving.

Anxiety becomes an issue when you're driving *and* you're thinking: *Oh my gosh, in thirty minutes, so-and-so is coming to the house and I'm not ready!* or, *Oh my gosh, I can't believe that happened to me ten years ago!*

Another great example of this is snowboarding. When I'm snowboarding all I can think about is my board and my edges. I always feel so calm at the end of a day of snowboarding because I wasn't thinking about a million things, just two.

You need to create the schedule and then focus on that one task you have for that allotted time. You will be surprised by how productive you'll be and how much peace of mind you will have.

Redefine Worry: A Rocking Chair Goes Nowhere

Highly sensitive women tend to worry. It's not a negativity or a weakness. We want to be sensitive to others' feelings and want to make everything nice-nice and not create conflict or hurt feelings. We can't control other people. Just like when you get invited to a party, going back to the schedule, you can't be concerned about hurting someone's feelings if you can't make it to a party or it genuinely doesn't fit your schedule, or you're just really exhausted and staying home that day would mean taking care of yourself.

Worrying isn't the right response, but while we were growing up most of us were taught that it is. So if Mom was a worrier — maybe she was highly sensitive like my mom was — you were probably taught that you should really worry about other people's feelings, and worry if your kids don't come home by the exact minute they said they would, or worry if you're hurting Aunt So-

and-So's feelings because you can't make it to that party.

When you start taking care of yourself and your needs, being the best woman that you can be, you will find that you will worry less, and you will start to trust that you taking care of yourself and being the best version of yourself is good enough, and you will let everybody else waste all their time worrying.

For a long time, I thought worrying was being productive. I thought worrying was actually doing something. Being a type A, I felt like I had to be active all the time.

So even while doing other things, I put a lot of energy into my thoughts: *Oh my gosh, I really hope the business grows this month!* and, *Oh my gosh, I really hope my kids grow up to feel content and live their gifts!*

My coach said to me, "I want you to visualize yourself sitting in a rocking chair, and you're rocking back and forth, back and forth."

For anyone who knows what it's like to sit in a rocking chair, you know that for all that movement you get nowhere. All you do is rock back and forth.

Then my coach said, "When you're rocking back and forth, I want you to think about your productivity. Where is all this rocking getting you? Are you going to get to the store by rocking back and forth in a rocking chair?"

Thinking that you might actually get to the store or go somewhere sitting in a rocking chair is like some version of insanity, right?

Worry is the same way. Worry's like sitting in a rocking chair all day long, thinking you're going to get somewhere.

So when my coach told me that, I thought: *Well, I'm not going to do that anymore, because I want to be productive. I definitely want to reach my full potential in this life. I'm not going to get there expending really good energy in the direction of worrying, because it doesn't actually do anything.*

I hope this visual helps you get rid of some of the guilt. Whether it's guilt or worry, it has the same effect on you. We talk a lot about guilt in Irish, Jewish, and Catholic traditions, but guilt has no color or religion. It does not discriminate. Everyone's got it.

To release your worry:

- Learn to recognize it.
- See where it came from.
- Say: *Thank you, no thank you.*

When I practiced letting go of worry, I freed up so much energy. All that energy now goes back into my schedule, and I get more done. It's a really huge piece of life learning.

Deep Breathing

When highly sensitive women get nervous or over-stimulated — which happens all the time — the way to bring yourself back to yourself is actually to breathe deeply. Dr. Andrew Weil promotes a five-minute breathing technique that I tried and it really worked. But it would take five minutes to do, and I didn't have five minutes.

So I use the shortcut version.

Action Item

I call this Buddha Belly Breaths.

1. Sit down with uncrossed legs.

2. Close your eyes.

3. Stick your belly out by relaxing your abdominal muscles. Ever notice how you try to "suck it in" all day? Man, that's a lot of wasted energy.

4. Breathe in through your nose, letting your belly fill with air.

5. Breathe out through your mouth and when you exhale, slowly let out all the air.

6. Say to yourself:
   On the inhale I breathe in peace.
   On the exhale I breathe out worry and overwhelm.

If your kids are having a temper tantrum, if you're overwhelmed and getting thrown off your schedule, take deep breaths like this. You can even do ten of them: in through the nose, out through the mouth. It will calm the mind.

This can work for kids too. It definitely keeps you present. This can work if you're in traffic (keep your eyes open in that case!), or if you just got over-stimulated by your boss or a client.

Your breathing connects you to your spirit. A mentor taught me this and I love it. Often when you're feeling anxious, worried, or nervous, it's because you're taking shallow breaths. You've disconnected from your spirit. You feel off-center: Nobody else understands. You can't put your finger on it. You just need to reconnect. As a highly sensitive woman, staying connected to your spirit is really important. It's another step toward unleashing yourself and maximizing your full potential.

If you're feeling off and you don't know why, try taking deep breaths. Reconnect to your spirit.

DON'T OVERTHINK IT

Highly sensitive women are thinkers. We're just thinkers by nature! It is so easy for you to get caught up in overthinking a decision. Many of my clients do this. Overthinking can happen when you're making a decision, or a purchase, or wonder if you're on the right life path.

If you're overthinking all the time, it's a lot of wasted energy. I'm all about energy conservation and putting energy in a forward direction. When you're overthinking, you're not in a forward direction; you're scattered. Energy is dissipating everywhere. You have to keep it simple. If you know that you're in the habit of overthinking, you can learn to catch yourself.

There Are No Mistakes

We need to redefine what a mistake really is: an opportunity to learn. When I started doing this with my children, I found that they were more excited to go out and try things.

Seeing mistakes as chances to learn changes your attitude:

- Life gets lighter.
- You're able to let your creativity out.
- You have a new curiosity about life.
- You take more risks.
- You gain peace of mind.

You're not bogged down in the negative downward-spiraling feelings of being a loser if you get it wrong. I taught my kids that since there are no mistakes, there's no such thing as failure. It's really you just trying and experimenting. When that's the case, it really helps you find out what it is you're meant to do with your life in this world.

When you're stuck in not wanting to make mistakes, there's a very tight feeling in the body. I'm sure you're experiencing it while reading this. I bet you can even remember that mistake you made that you've been grilled on for so many years by your mother or guardian or teacher or coach. It's amazing how easily that stuff comes to mind.

When I really started to believe that everything in life has value and meaning, my whole life changed. Now I'm more excited to go out and try new things. That belief opened me up to take more risks, which is what you need to unleash yourself and maximize your potential.

I've heard it said that life really happens outside your comfort zone. It happens in the process of making mistakes too.

When my son comes home from winning a lot of chess tournaments, I say to him, "Luke, you haven't lost yet? Come on! Play someone better than you!"

I tell him, "Every time you lose, you learn something big, so go lose to someone and then tell me what you learned, so that next time you can win again."

He gets a chuckle out of it now. It is really important that we redefine failure. When we talk in our household about failure, it's a really light conversation. It's actually somewhat comedic. I think that's how life should be, if you want to maximize your potential.

The Past Belongs in the Past

For highly sensitive women, it is very easy to get caught up in reliving the past. You may think that what happened in the past is who you are. But really, you're evolving better and better versions of yourself, year after year after year.

You may feel hesitant to take the next big step, or get into a relationship, or start that business.

That thought comes up: *Oh, well, last time I tried to meet someone or turn that idea into a business, it didn't work.*

You immediately shut down any creative juices that might be bubbling up. You have left the present moment.

Remember:

- Keep it simple.
- Be in the present moment.

When you stay in the present, you can't have anxiety and worry (because they are all about what was or what will be). You can be the best version of yourself only when you stay in the present moment.

I'm not a huge fan of talk therapy. The more we talk about our past, the more we bring ourselves into the past.

So while I am a fan of talking about and knowing where you came from, at some point, it's time to move forward. Here's one way to make that happen.

Action Item

Write a letter to yourself:

Dear Self,

I love you.

I'm sorry for all the hurts and years you spent dwelling on them.

You did your best.

Love,

Me

Then burn the letter and move on, because the past belongs in the past.

I promise you, if you focus on where you're headed and find your own ways of making peace with your past, your whole life will open up for you.

It's different for everyone. Some people are more highly sensitive than others. You may feel that sitting around and thinking about stuff doesn't help you process your past.

You may sense your ability to process is helped by physical activity:

- Taking a yoga class
- Running
- Hiking or simply being in nature

Or try getting bodywork or therapy from a trained practitioner:

- Massage therapist
- Acupuncturist
- Reiki healer
- Neurolinguistic programmer (NLP)

When you find the best way for you to process that stuff, you can really leave your past in the past. For us highly sensitive women, and really for everybody from my experience, just talking about stuff doesn't get it done. To leave your past in the past, you have to experience what you need to, and then move on—and don't overthink it!

**Trust Your Intuition
(Higher Power, Higher Knowing)**

This is a big piece for us highly sensitive peeps! I find trusting intuition is the first thing to go when a highly sensitive woman is out of balance. We stop trusting and looking outside ourselves for answers when normally, truth be told, we are so in touch with ourselves.

Repeat after me: *I always know what is best for me.*

Get in touch with that part of you so you can hear the answers. Maybe you're wondering what exactly *is* your intuition.

Your intuition is that little voice that talks to you:

- First thing in the morning
- Right before bed
- Before you're about to make a really big decision

Your little voice talks to you. Some people call it *the crazy voice*, but I think they're crazy for thinking it's the crazy voice. It's actually the voice in you that knows more than you, more than what your conscious brain knows. I call your higher power your *higher knowing*. The more you can use your intuition to guide you, the easier life becomes and the more you're in the flow and decisions come more easily.

I use this one all the time, especially with three small kids in the house. For instance, everyone's got their kids in nine thousand after school activities. I just trust my inner knowing that that is not what my kids need. No judgment if you want to do it!

My intuition tells me that my kids need downtime, just like I do.

"Let kids be kids, and I swear it's going to work out for the best."

You've just got to trust, especially when it's tricky and you're the only one, or one of just a few, making a big decision. And in the case of being a mom and going against the norm, *definitely* lean on your intuition.

Writing this book was an exercise in trust for me. I can easily talk about trusting your intuition in business. I have a lot of confidence in that. But jumping on board to write a book—that felt like some scary stuff to me!

When I met with the publishers, however, my intuition just said: "Go for it!"

My intuition told me, "It's your time. The money will come. The time to write the book will come. The people who need to read the book will read it, and you will effect change the way you want to, on a larger scale, without having to be necessarily one-on-one with people."

There's only so much time, and as highly sensitive women, we need our downtime!

My intuition was urging me to do more in the world, but it was also telling me, "There's only so much time you have, because you know you can get overwhelmed easily, especially with the kids and the life and the husband and the business and the house."

So I turned down many other opportunities that came my way until one came that felt just right. There it was: it presented itself, I jumped on board, and I haven't looked back. That's how it works.

And just like a muscle, the more you work it out the more toned it becomes. The same is true for your intuition. The more you dial in, the more you are able to hear yourself clearly!

JOLIE'S TESTIMONIAL

I sought Jenn out because I was having a lot of trouble managing the different areas of my life; family, business, personal. I wanted to get my business off the ground, but kept getting held back by my other roles. I was looking for some structure and organizational tools.

Jenn from the outset made me feel empowered, as if there was no way I wouldn't knock it out of the park. I spoke to her for thirty minutes and at the end of the conversation, I knew she was my woman.

I've been working with Jenn for several months now, and she has exceeded my expectations. How? I came for A, B, and C, and I've gotten A *through* Z. I have managed to eat well, organize my family life, get a company off the ground, and make a plan for finishing my book. I'm indebted to her.

I'm big on examples, so here's one. The other day, I had been coming off a rough week, kids were sick, house was falling apart; I wanted to toss in the towel. I wanted to give up on all I had started and put into motion, thinking there was no way I could do it all. Then I spoke with Jenn and got that fresh perspective I've come to love and appreciate, and I kept on going!

~ Jolie Andreoni
Writer, Mom, & Founder
www.EnchantedChambers.com

CHAPTER
THREE

Find Your Focus by Kickin' the Sugar

If you really want to do something you'll find a way. If you don't, you'll find an excuse.

~ Jim Rohn

Sugar addiction has become an epidemic. Almost everyone I know is struggling to get sugar out of their diet and keep it out at a manageable level. When I meet people interested in working with me, I'll ask about their diets. Often people talk about how much crap they eat, or their nighttime cravings, or how they have to have their wine at night. Some even say they're just plain addicted to sugar.

Processed foods and sugar are pretty high on the list of things people eat every day. It has also become commonplace to have sugar and carb cravings. Many people don't know the way out, and it's ripping them away from their ability to focus and live a healthy, juiced-up life.

If what you're eating doesn't get addressed, then it's very difficult to find your focus and feel good in your body. Additionally, people exert a lot of wasted energy on trying the latest diet fad and over-exercising. They can't figure out what is really causing the weight gain, zapping their energy, and stealing their focus.

When I help people get the sugar out and give them tools to kick the cravings, they're able to find their focus and energy without being dependent on outside sources like caffeine. They get in touch with what they want from their lives—not from some outside source, but from deep within themselves.

Amazingly enough, they also have a newfound, unshakable level of confidence as the brainfog starts to clear. It is pretty awesome to witness.

SUGAR'S EFFECT ON THE MIND, BODY, AND SPIRIT

We hear all the time from health experts, "Don't eat sugar. It's not good for you."

I'm sure your mom used to say, "It will rot your teeth."

As highly sensitive women, we are even more affected by the white powdery stuff. No one ever really talks about how sugar affects our ability to feel good about ourselves or the way it blocks us from that radiant energy we all want and deserve! Sugar clearly affects the mind, the body, and the spirit. When I started making that connection with myself and then with clients, they all really wanted to get the sugar out; not because it was something bad, not because it would rot their teeth. Their desire to get rid of sugar even transcended their desire to lose weight.

They knew if they could kick the sugar habit, they could have clear thoughts, get creative, and feel good. Sugar in the body really suppresses us on so many levels.

Sugar is known to cause many problems:

- **A depressed immune system, causing us to get sick more often:** There's a direct correlation between holiday season and flu season. People eat way too much sugar for long periods of time, so the virus is able to take hold in the body and make you sick— very sick.

- **Mental confusion:** We see this as "normal" and something that coffee can fix.

- **Anxiety and depression:** For people who struggle with these things, there's usually a huge sugar addiction or a carb addiction that coincides. There's definitely something related to sugar. When I get clients off of sugar, I notice they start feeling more themselves—their real selves. They are not anxious and overwhelmed easily, but calm, relaxed, and centered.

Confusion: the Mind

When you eat sugar, something happens, especially if you're a highly sensitive woman.

Sugar affects your ability:

- To focus
- To think clearly
- To know what you want
- To be able to really tap into your intuition

It simply dulls everything.

Processed foods and sugar drinks sprinkled throughout the day causes blood sugar to spike and then drop. As your blood sugar drops, you will get that 3:00 p.m. crash everyone knows all too well. This comes along with mental confusion, caused by less fuel going to the brain. You will probably be even more tired than before you ate or drank the stuff.

Do this over a long period of time, day after day, week after week, and month after month, year after year, and you'll be on a perpetual rollercoaster of mixed emotions and mental confusion.

Been there. Done that.

If you're reading this and think: *Wait, I eat sugar and I'm not confused, walking around in some state of crazy that you're talking about!*

Yes, that's probably true. Now go ahead and try

my Jenn's 21-Day Reclaim Your Mojo Clean Eating Challenge (which I'll describe in detail later). And *then* tell me how you feel! It's a whole new world fo' sure.

I've seen my women clients who complete the challenge and continue to eat clean feel the difference:

- They think more clearly.
- They feel like life has a new excitement.
- They're able to really plan and organize.

It's really amazing to see.

Getting sugar out and knowing how to get it *back* out once it creeps back in is a game changer for unleashing yourself. A focused woman on a mission, off sugar, is unstoppable. If you're looking to focus and take your life to the next level, this is an essential step.

Inflammation: The Body

You want to get the sugar out because of how it affects the body. It is one of the biggest culprits in causing inflammation in the body. Inflammation takes on many symptoms.

Some of the most common symptoms are:

- Achy joints, arthritis in severe cases
- Asthma
- Allergies
- Headaches
- Chronic fatigue

- Digestive trouble
- High blood pressure
- Inability to stabilize blood sugar
- Constipation
- Diarrhea
- Skin problems

The more severe cases include:

- Depression
- Diabetes
- Cancer

Most people don't put two and two together. They don't realize that sugar is a huge factor in their symptoms. They think it's something they need to just live with or worse yet, take a drug to cure. The drug only masks the underlying inflammation, which acts more like a Band-aid than a cure.

Now, when I say sugar, let me be crystal clear. By sugar I mean *all* sugar, organic or not, and most sweeteners.

The most common are:

- Table sugar
- Brown sugar
- Sugar in the Raw
- Turbinado sugar
- Honey
- Maple sugar
- Barley malt

- Agave
- Cane sugar
- Rice syrup
- Dextrose
- Fructose
- Glucose
- Any word that ends in "ose"

I find stevia to be okay in small quantities, but only you will know if it is okay for you when you have it and see how your body reacts. My family and I love having pure Vermont maple syrup on our homemade pancakes and that doesn't seem to trigger us for more sweets all day long.

You will know best, so explore what works for you.

And don't get me started on that artificial crap:

- Aspartame
- Splenda
- Equal
- Whatever the latest artificial sweetener might be

These sweeteners are known to trick the body by not raising your blood sugar levels, but trust me when I tell you the body is smarter than that. Artificial sweeteners of all kinds are toxic to the body. They store in your fat cells and only contribute to making you fatter and sicker. Yup. They slow down your metabolism.

Here's a hint I give my clients to tell if something is

real or not: if you can't pronounce the ingredients, then don't eat it. Also, most people don't know that 4 grams of sugar = 1 teaspoon of sugar; so before you reach for that so-called breakfast bar that is 20 grams of sugar, understand that's like eating 5 teaspoons of sugar with no minerals or vitamins, only empty calories that rob the body and do not contribute to its well-being.

You may not realize what happens in the body when you eat processed food like sugary baked goods, 100-calorie packs of chemicals and sugar, or fried foods that have had their nutritional structure altered by high heat.

Rather than getting into all the terminology that so many people get into — the science behind it — I'm just going to tell you when you eat something that's not good for the body, the body has a protective mechanism that will cause it to swell to protect itself. The body takes on water.

Then there is the matter of weight and that oh-so-devilish thing we use to measure our "dieting" success, also known as the scale.

Maybe you've indulged in a big meal and now you notice:

- You're feeling bloated and you can't button your pants.
- Your joints hurt the day after.
- You experience the infamous: *How did I put on three pounds in one day?*

It's not because what you ate stored as fat within the last twenty-four hours, but because you ate things that were harmful to the body and the body took on water to protect itself. You've basically eaten things that are inflaming your body. Your best bet is to start figuring out what those foods are, and get those foods out of your diet for as long as it takes the body to repair itself and not bloat from eating them.

My Mojo Challenge is a great first step to resetting the body, and a detox is the second great step. I find it's too harsh on the body to go straight from eating junk to detoxing. Eating cleaner first eases the body into the whole idea of living a cleaner life. I'll talk about this more in a little bit.

Stifling Emotions: The Spirit

A lot of women I know struggle with cravings that tend to come on hard at night.

Clients tell me, "I've been good all day and then at night, I just can't stop eating."

Or they feel successful in every other area of life, but for some reason, when it comes to food and sweets or even salty foods like chips, they just can't stop.

From my work with clients and my own work as a recovering sugar-a-holic, I've noticed when we get cravings for sugar, especially at night, it usually means there's something from an emotional standpoint that's trying to come up. Even after clients get all the physiological stuff in balance in their bodies, cravings might still be hanging around. Maybe there's an emotion or a thought that's trying to come up, or a change that is needed in your life that you've been ignoring.

At night I believe your emotional body wakes up and if you eat sugar at that precise moment, you suppress whatever it is that's trying to come up. And if you truly believe that we are spiritual beings living in a material world, then you will start to be able to connect with what the spirit is telling you through those cravings.

I now use my cravings as a guide for my life. When they are really powerful at night I always stop and check in and do the exercise I'm about to share. Then I correct my course the following week. It has helped me make so many changes in my life, and I hope it does the same for you.

Action Item

For one or two nights, when the cravings hit, don't give in.

Don't eat the food you're craving. Just sit and notice and see and feel what comes up.

Rather than trying to figure it out, get in the moment.

When you're having the cravings and the cookies are screaming from the cabinet, "You've been good all day. You deserve a treat," or my all-time favorite, "You'll only have one cookie; how bad could that be?" don't give in.

Sit there and just notice:

- What's bugging you?
- What's out of balance?
- Who upset you today?
- What change needs to happen?
- Take out a pen and paper and write down what comes up.

I can guarantee you that you'll be amazed, maybe even elated, about what actually arises.

This is an important exercise for getting past the cravings and getting off of sugar for the long term. You won't be doing it because you're motivated, or because you have lots of self-control, but because now you're really starting to understand how your emotions play into your cravings.

CRAVINGS ARE YOUR FRIEND

Getting a handle on your cravings is an integral part of unleashing yourself and creating radiant energy and unshakeable confidence. There is so much energy wasted on cravings. Women in particular expend so much energy on the food they eat, especially the foods that they think will make them fat.

I talk about cravings from a different angle than using willpower, deprivation, or denial to get past them. Anyone reading this book who has had cravings knows that willpower does not work in the long term. One bad day in the office or one sleepless night with the kids and wham-o! You're eating that favorite treat that you've denied yourself all those days.

Cravings Tell You Something Needs to Change

So many women I know think cravings are something negative. Cravings aren't a negative or something taboo. Cravings are a sign that something is going on;

it could be physiological if your diet and eating habits are poor, or it could be something emotional bringing them on. When clients tell me that had to have the wine or those cookies last night, I want to know more.

If you have cravings, here are some questions you can ask yourself:

Am I running around too much during the day and using sugar at night to unwind?

Am I lacking nonfood treats all day that then turn to food treats at night?

(A spiced-up life has no room for sugar, I like to say!)

Am I holding my tongue at work, coming home feeling frustrated, then taking it out on that pint of Ben and Jerry's ice cream?

If you can look at cravings as your road map, they will take on a whole new meaning. You can view cravings as a way to start looking at your life from a fresh perspective.

When they come up, you need to look at how you operate in your life and your business, how you operate as a parent, partner, spouse, husband, wife, employee, or employer. You will almost welcome cravings and start welcoming the changes that you're going to start making.

To Give In or Not to Give In

Ah, this is the question: To give in or not to give in; my clients ask about this all the time.

"Jenn, I don't know. I gave in, I didn't know if I should."

"I didn't give in and now I'm miserable."

Only you will know when to give in and when not to. With that said, the little asterisk is that if you're feeling addicted and disempowered by the cravings you're having, it's probably a good idea not to give in. Take it as a sign that something needs to change.

When I'm out with my family on vacation and we're having a great time, the kids might have some yummy homemade ice cream. I sometimes get cravings, but it's not a craving for the ice cream. It's a craving to just be there with my family and enjoy the same foods, and just have a good time. That is when I give in.

It's maybe a subtle difference to you, but the defining piece is what I go back to in every one of these chapters:

How do you feel?

Do you feel good giving in, or does it make you feel bad and disempowered?

When it's a good feeling, I do it. When I know something's off and I know I'm going to feel bad or not-so-empowered later, I don't give in, I check in.

Making Peace with Cravings

Cravings are like a tug-of-war. You tug on one end; cravings tug on the other end. You tug; cravings tug. If you played tug-of-war as a kid, you know the harder you tug, the harder that other person or people are going to be tugging. It's just what tug-of-war is about.

People treat their cravings like their opponent in a tug-of-war. The best, most simplistic way to get past them is to drop the mental tug-of-war. Drop it, and be Zen-like.

I have an organic garden, and the weeds are my nemesis. A gardener who's been around a long time saw me getting frustrated with my lack of progress with pulling weeds.

I'll never forget what he said: "You need to be Zen with the weeds."

It just hit me like a ton of bricks: It's the same thing for cravings. You know the weeds are going to come, because that's part of having an organic garden. Just like you know cravings are going to come, because it's just part of living and being in and out of balance with the body.

You can't stay in perfect balance all the time. Being in perfect balance is getting out of balance. If you know that's going to be the case, you can drop the rope and make peace whichever way you can. That is a huge part of making friends with your cravings, and not trying to avoid them or living in fear that they are going to come back.

A lot of women have a fear around the return of their cravings. But when you get rid of the fear, you can actually start to feel empowered; you have power over them because you're no longer struggling with them.

Think of how you treat a friend. Would you treat a friend by beating them up and cursing them and being angry and pissed off and not wanting to see them at night? No! If cravings were your friend, you would love them. You would hug them. You would embrace them. In return what you would get is a lessening of cravings. I promise. I guarantee it!

HOW TO KICK IT AND MANAGE IT LONG TERM

The day I learned how to kick the cravings was the day I got my life back. Once I did that I went on a mission to help anyone and everyone who would listen. It is not about getting off sugar forever once you learn how to kick the cravings. Let's be honest. Well, not unless you live in a cave away from all civilization and holidays. Come on. Who doesn't live in the United States and have a piece of pie on Thanksgiving? It's about knowing how to get off the white powdery stuff once you're back on it with sanity, calm, and confidence.

What Are You Committed to?

It takes energy to make changes.

It takes energy to lose weight.

It takes energy to make a baby.

It takes energy to start a business.

It takes energy to heal.

You can do Weight Watchers or Jenny Craig or one of those cookie-cutter diet programs. But most people revert back to their old diet, including sugar. It's almost as if when someone stopped looking over your shoulder, you stopped *being good*. You were not driven from within to make those changes. It was coming from some external force. It's because some core beliefs didn't get identified and changed.

In order to create lasting change, step one of the process needs to be creating the belief in you that you matter. You're worthy. Once you have that internalized, you will start to find time in your day for yourself to do what it takes to kick the sugar

You will see from Jenn's 21-day Reclaim Your Mojo Clean Eating Challenge that it takes effort to plan ahead and cook and eat cleaner meals. That's part of what it takes to kick sugar. No one can do it for you.

You have to start with some affirming words to tell yourself because the journey to kicking sugar is a journey you will be on for the rest of your life.

> ### Action Item
>
> Write affirming words on some sticky notes and put them around the house:
>
> - *I matter.*
> - *I make time for myself.*
> - *I make time to slow down.*
> - *When I fall down, I choose to get up and try again.*
> - *I cannot fail.*
> - *I will be open to new ideas.*
> - *I trust the process.*
>
> Put them in your wallet to be read every day. *Every day.*

Whatever it takes to commit to thinking a little differently is the whole objective prior to starting your twenty-one-day challenge. If you want things to be different, you have to do different things.

Redefining Stress in Your Life

We've got to talk about redefining stress if we're *ever* going to kick cravings and learn how to get off of sugar. Say you've done a cleanse, some sort of detox, or some sort of program where you've kicked the sugar temporarily. Then stress comes in with emotional triggers and then you go right back to sugar.

You have to take a look at stressors:

- You're planning too much to get done in one day.

- You have clients or customers whom you allow to drain your energy. (You know it's a choice. No one has the power to drain you.)

- You hold your tongue rather than tell people what you really think because you are afraid of hurting their feelings.

If you don't start taking a look at your relationship to that stress, you'll be able to kick cravings in spurts, but you'll never feel comfortable having it out for any substantial amount of time.

Take a look at what your triggers are in your life that cause you stress:

- Things that get your goat
- People who push your buttons
- Stuff that pisses you off and angers you

It used to be that if someone cut me off while driving, I'd blow my top. I felt undone by all this rudeness in the world. I had to take a longer look at what the hell was going on.

Why would I allow that to pull me off center and upset me?

Truth be told, I had no idea what's going on in the lives of any of those people. For all I know their mother was in the hospital and they were rushing to see her. I choose to no longer let someone else affect my day. I wasn't going to take it out on myself any longer and eat a row of cookies that night to soothe myself in some artificial way.

My wise Uncle Pete once told me, "Don't make other people's problems your problems."

Love that one. Let others have their problems. There is no need to make them yours.

Take a look at your stress:

What raises your heart rate?

What gets you angry?

What causes you to feel like a cookie will make it all better?

Review your priorities for yourself, your kids, and your family, and your business if you've got one. Start redefining them so that you can have the time and energy to devote to yourself and what it will take to kick those cravings.

Reclaim Your Mojo

While I've said a lot of nice, fancy stuff up until now, trust me: I'm as straight as it gets when it comes time to show you the money, to tell you how to kick it.

Here's the thing: What you need to know is that it is doable on your own, even though one of the steps is to get support. Everything is better with support if you ask me, but what matters most is that you're committed to change and discover new things about yourself and your body.

Sometimes people are hesitant because the problem has been going on for so long that they think there's no hope. One woman I met was trying to kick cravings for, I think, it must have been about thirty years. I told her I guaranteed I could help her finally kick the habit.

She said, "How am I going to not trust that?"

She joined one of my Challenges, followed the steps, and within twenty-one days she called me in tears of joy and told me that she was able to kick them. So without further ado, here's the condensed version of Jenn's 21-Day Reclaim Your Mojo Clean Eating Challenge.

For more support and to sign up for the official Challenge with my undivided attention, you can visit:

www.jenneddencoaching.com

Number One: Eat a protein-rich breakfast within about one hour of waking. I prefer you eat enough to get you through to lunch, but if you're like me and require a mid-morning snack that's okay; just make sure it's food and not some chemicalized wrapped wanna-be food. If you work out very early in the morning (like 6:00) I find it's okay to work out first and then make sure you eat within about thirty minutes of your workout.

A lot of people start their day with a cup of coffee and then don't eat breakfast until 10:00, at which point it's a yogurt or a bagel or a breakfast bar — something that causes your blood sugar levels to spike.

First thing in the morning, you want:

- To watch what you're putting in your mouth
- To read ingredients
- To have a solid protein breakfast

How much protein should you have?

I tend to shy away from exact amounts because every body is different. My recommendation is to adjust as you go and see what feels good for your body.

Here are three possible breakfasts:

- 2 organic eggs
  ½ avocado sliced
  handful of cherry tomatoes

- 3 Applegate Farms turkey breakfast sausages

½ avocado
handful of organic strawberries

- Vegan protein shake (high quality; no soy and no protein isolates) blended with organic frozen berries
  ice
  water
  ½ avocado to thicken, if you like

Sometimes if I'm still hungry after breakfast I'll add the protein shake to breakfast so that I feel satiated before starting my day.

The number one goal is to eat real food without the refined carbohydrates that will spike blood sugar. Note for those who eats grains in the morning: I find them to be harsh on the body first thing and for sure they can cause cravings later. So for experimental purposes take them out during the challenge and check in on those cravings.

For a complete list of foods and meal ideas visit:

www.jecoaching.com/bookoffer/mojomealssnacksandmore

For a list of frequently asked Mojo Challenge questions, visit:

www.jecoaching.com/bookoffer/frequentlyaskedquestionsmojochallenge

Number Two: Eat three to five meals a day depending on your hunger levels. They will vary from day to day and season to season, so adjust as you go.

The worst thing to do is skip meals. It causes your blood sugar to swing. Later in the day, you're going to get cravings because of the imbalance.

Here are some examples of good meals:

- Organic free-range chicken
  Steamed broccoli with Himalayan sea salt

- Wild-caught salmon cooked in extra virgin olive oil (EVOO)
  String beans in garlic powder and sea salt

- ½ sweet potato, baked
  Black beans or lentils with ½ avocado, salsa, grape tomatoes, cilantro (I used organic canned beans that I simply rinse off and eat)

Mojo snacks include:

- Hummus and organic cucumbers, sliced
- Handful of raw, unsalted nuts
- Raw almond butter and organic celery

Many times cravings come from the chemicals in processed foods. They're designed to give us cravings. Yup.

So in your choosing your foods, I want you to eat:

- Organic
- Wild caught
- Free range
- Chemical-free

As much as possible, strive for those foods. You can check out the environmental working group at www.ewg.org for an updated list of the twelve foods that should be organic and the fifteen foods that are okay to be conventional. Your goal is to eat as many one-ingredient foods during the challenge as possible. This will help you tremendously with cravings.

Number Three: Drink clean, filtered water as your primary source of fluids. Caffeinated beverages and teas dehydrate you, so they don't count. Most people walk around dehydrated and they don't even know it.

Start your day with a full glass of filtered water if you can. You need to hydrate. It's a known fact that our bodies are between 60 and 80 percent water, so you can imagine what happens when you're walking around dehydrated. Drink your water. And when it comes to what water to drink, feel free to do your own research. I've been told by experts that Poland Spring water contains chlorine that calcifies your thyroid—so be careful. Not all water is created equal. At time of print of this book I found that Fiji Water, bottled outside the United States, is a safe source of bottled water.

A good rule of thumb is to consume half the number of pounds of your body weight in ounces of water: a 120-pound woman should drink about sixty ounces. But I say go with your body. See how you feel. I was drinking up to a gallon a day at one point, and I was really feeling good.

Do you have a very active lifestyle and sweat a lot?

You lose a lot of water and electrolytes through sweating, so keep that in mind and definitely skip those sugary sports drinks. They have so much sugar they don't actually hydrate you. They inflame you instead.

Drink clean, filtered water. If you feel like you need a mineral boost you can cook with seaweed in your soups and rice (although for the challenge you are not adding rice back yet).

The quality of the water really does matter. Either you drink clean filtered water or your liver and kidneys are going to do the filtering for you! I personally have a whole-house system to filter out the garbage but you decide what's best for you.

Number Four: No white foods or anything processed. I'm not kidding! *No white food* and this includes white potatoes. Sweet potatoes are okay in moderation. It's absolutely amazing what happens to the body when you take white food out of your diet. All of it. You will actually start to notice you won't crave it as much and then you won't crave it at all.

I'm talking about getting out the gluten-free stuff, too. While I'm an advocate of living with less gluten in our lives, I am not an advocate of all the chemicals and sugar that can go along with living a gluten-free life. Just because those pretzels are gluten free doesn't mean they are any better for you than the wheat ones. Read the labels. You will be amazed at how much garbage is in there.

During the challenge, you will not eat:

- Breads
- Chips
- Crackers
- Cakes
- All that white stuff that comes in packages

You want it off your menu.

For a complete shopping list, recipes, and meal ideas, visit:

www.jecoaching.com/bookoffer/ mojomealssnacksandmore

Number Five: No fruit with the exception of:

- Organic strawberries
- Organic blueberries
- Organic green apples (red are okay too)

These particular fruits are low in sugar and process slower in the body than melons, for instance.

Number Six: No dairy. This is a biggie for people: no pasteurized, homogenized dairy. It is almost unbelievable, but when you start taking dairy out, the body actually starts to shrink. It makes sense if you think about it: a calf becomes a two-ton cow by drinking it's mama's milk! Did you know we are the only mammals that drink another mammal's milk? Maybe, just maybe, we shouldn't be drinking it.

Most people don't think of it that way, but I want you to. In our family, we don't drink cow's milk. We have ice cream on occasion for sure, but milk, yogurt, and cheese are not a daily occurrence. Goat milk might be okay for you but until the cravings subside, I want it out. Same for raw milk: There are wonderful benefits associated with raw milk, but for experimental purposes let's keep it simple and take all dairy out. Just so I'm clear: when I say *no dairy* I mean no butter, no cow's milk, no hard cheese or soft cheese, no cottage cheese and clearly no ice cream, nothing that comes from a cow.

The one cheese that is low in lactose and doesn't seem to affect those who consume it in small quantities is parmesan cheese. So go ahead and include a little on your food if you'd like. If you're not feeling energized after a few days, take that out for experimental purposes.

Number Seven: Find a few good meals and repeat them. Just keep it simple because I know you're busy, and you like to do things simply like I do. So find a few good meals and snacks and repeat them for twenty-one days. I promise it becomes almost comforting to eat simple, quick meals that take less than about twenty minutes to prepare.

For a list of foods and meal ideas visit:

www.jecoaching.com/bookoffer/
mojomealssnacksandmore

Number Eight: Get enough sleep. This is a huge one. Cravings will not—I repeat—*will not* go away if you don't get enough sleep. They always say to get seven to nine hours; you can round it off somewhere in the eight range. Your body will know. If you don't do that, your body's not detoxing properly at night, which is very important for overall health.

Secondly, if you don't get enough rest you will be looking for sugar to give you quick energy. Not to mention you have hormones in your body that regulate appetite—yes, we do. When we're not sleeping, the regulatory appetite-suppressing hormone (also known as ghrelin) is out of whack and the satiating hormone (also known as leptin) is also out of whack. It is not uncommon to want to eat everything, and the kitchen sink, because the signal between your brain and stomach is not working well.

Number Nine: Take a good probiotic. The standard American diet (SAD) is:

- High in refined sugar
- Excessive in poor-quality animal protein
- High in chemicals
- Low in organic fresh vegetables
- Low in lacto-fermented foods (sauerkraut, kimchi)

All this stuff can disrupt the balance of the bacteria in your gut. Your gut is where your immune system resides. As well, a majority of serotonin is made there, which is needed for positive mental health. All probiotics are not created equal.

Here is what I want you to look for:

- High Culture Content: at least 10 billion cultures in one capsule
- Number of strains: the more the better

For the latest recommendations on what I have found to be effective you can always check out my website at www.jenneddencoaching.com and click on the *Shop* tab. I tend to recommend only what my family and I are using and consider highly effective!

Number Ten: Take one day per week off from the challenge, preferably the same day, and on a weekend so as to not feel deprived.

Now, do you *need* to take a day off?

Hell no.

Do I think you'll *want* to take a day off until you get the swing of this?

Absolutely.

On that day off, eat whatever you want.

Some people say, "Oh my God, don't tell me that! I will eat all junk food."

I say go ahead, but take note of how you feel the next day. Start making the connection between your low energy and crazy cravings and specific junk food you're eating.

If the following week you decide you don't want that one day off, and it's not out of willpower or deprivation, tell yourself: *I'm not going to do it.*

It's because you frigging want to *feel good*! So give yourself a day off, and then see how you feel.

Number Eleven: Move. Move like your life depends on it, 'cause it does. I need you to add movement to your life if you're more sedentary than you'd like to be. It's really important that your body has the opportunity to detox. To get toxins moving out of the body, you've got to sweat.

Plus, those little hormones we have called *endorphins* really kick in when you start to move. They make you feel good. That helps kick cravings too, just by getting you to feel better. And I will mention quickly that if you don't have a weight-lifting routine or some routine around building muscle, please put it on your to-do list in the near future. There is nothing better than having muscle on your body to keep the weight off, as well as help give you energy during the day and into the later years.

Did you know that muscle burns more calories at rest than fat, so a lean person stays leaner just by having more muscle on them?

Yep.

Number Twelve: No alcohol. It really taxes the liver and causes sugar cravings, especially my red- and white-wine drinkers.

After all, wine is grapes, right?

And grapes are fruit and fruit has sugar. This one makes some people cringe.

Some people say, "Hmm, I've done cleanses and things where you can drink red wine," but I'm telling you: no alcohol.

No alcohol, except for your day off. See how you feel not having it so that when you add it back you can notice the changes. This one is a game changer for many.

Number Thirteen: Don't go it alone. This one is last but certainly not least. Ask a friend to join you so that you can compare notes on what's going on with your mood and how you feel eating differently, especially with getting the sugar out.

Remember: reaching out for support is a strength, not a weakness.

JANET'S TESTIMONIAL

In 2013 I began de-toxing from almost thirty years in Corporate America as a vice president of human resources. I was miserable—not in great shape and no energy. It was in 2014 when I first met Jenn. She had amazing energy—so down to earth—and also, she was in amazing shape—physically and mentally.

Working with Jenn was my missing link. While I had made some progress at the gym, I wasn't seeing the results I envisioned. Learning from Jenn how proper nutrition impacts *everything*, I started seeing incredible results physically. But equally as important, my whole mental outlook shifted too! I loved Jenn's 21-Day Mojo Clean Eating Challenge, and believe me, I got my Mojo back.

During this time I had so much clarity I launched a new business buying, fixing, and flipping houses and I got my real estate license as well. Jenn has taken on such an important role in my life. She is my life coach and I look forward to my weekly phone calls where I know I have that safe space without judgment to figure out what's next.

~ Janet Henderson
Real estate entrepreneur and very grateful
client of Jenn

CHAPTER
FOUR

Get Out the Junk

Out of clutter, find simplicity.
~ Albert Einstein

So often, clearing out and cleaning up your life is an overlooked part of unleashing yourself and maximizing your potential. You fall back into old patterns and you don't know why. It is liberating to get out the old to make room physically, mentally, and spiritually for the new. This chapter is all about making room for what is to come.

CLEARING YOUR PHYSICAL ENVIRONMENT

Our physical environment is often overlooked as something important and something that we should take seriously when we're thinking about our health and looking for radiant energy. It affects our focus and our energy—our vibration. People are willing to try the latest detox. They'll change their diets and even exercise more. Then they come home to that office of piled-high unopened mail and whatever they've put off making a decision about. They will not think twice about how that is affecting their health and energy.

Nothing keeps you stagnant like piles and piles of clutter in your physical environment.

Your physical environment includes:

- Your car
- Where you sleep
- Your bedroom
- Your office
- Your garage
- Your front porch or foyer

You may take for granted some of the spaces that could impact you, places that you either spend a lot of time in or see on a daily basis. Definitely pay special attention to where you're sleeping. When you clean out the stuff, you actually start to feel better, more focused, and more energized and you might even notice that you've started to sleep better. Clutter is stagnant energy from under your bed and you can't free yourself up if your physical environment is a mess.

A cluttered house equals a cluttered mind. While we can eat well and do all these other things to help us, if we don't clean out the physical environment, the other stuff never really sticks for the long-term.

You Are Your Environment

One of my clients was stuck on those last ten pounds of weight, and she was doing everything to a T. She was eating clean, working on her stress, weight training, and starting to take a look at her relationships.

At some point in the coaching, you've got to take a look at everything going on in your client's life.

"What are your closets like?" I asked.

"Ugh, I can't believe you asked me that!" she said. "They are packed to the gills with three different sizes of clothes that I've been wearing over the last ten years, depending on how much weight I had on or off."

"Okay, well if you want those last ten pounds off, we need to start cleaning out the clutter that's energetically surrounding you."

"Oh, Jenn, really?"

"Go do it, and come back in a week or two and let me know what happens."

She did it. She came back, and her weight started to move down again. She became a believer and I was reminded how important it is to clean out your environment.

Highly sensitive women are very much affected by not only food and the quality of it, but also by the physical environment. If you are highly sensitive, you will probably agree that you absorb energy. If you see things that are in disarray and not organized, you may find that you feel unfocused, sometimes even enraged.

It triggers something in you that makes you feel, well, kinda nutty.

It was true for me for many years. Then I started taking control of my environment, clearing stuff out and bringing order to my surroundings. I found that I could more consistently focus and feel good. We're talking about maximizing your potential; especially if you're a mom-entrepreneur like me, I only have so much time in a day to get my biz work done. Then I have my kid time, and my husband time, and my me time. So when I'm sitting, ready to work, I really want to be focused.

Pick a Room and Declutter

I'm all about then taking action, but in a way that is not overwhelming. When I talk with a lot of women about clutter, and they realize how much stuff they have, they get overwhelmed. Overwhelm causes people to freeze up and not take action.

As soon as you finish reading this section, put the book down and pick a room. Pick something you can declutter quickly — meaning maybe it would take a few hours but no longer than a full day — otherwise you'll lose momentum.

What you don't want to do is start decluttering, then have to pick the kids up, or talk with a client, or go on a trip, and it's left incomplete. It's very important when you're decluttering that you feel complete with that one section that you're working on. So if it's a closet, you make sure you have enough time in that day, or in those three hours, to complete that. The last thing you want to do is half-declutter; it really makes the head spin.

Pick the first thing that's bugging you. It might be your front hall closet, or your car. Go for what I call the *hottest button*, the thing that's bugging you the most, and go for it. Only you will know what needs to go first.

CLEANING UP YOUR RELATIONSHIPS

When we're talking about unleashing ourselves and having radiant energy and unshakable confidence, relationships are often overlooked. Take a look and see, from an energetic perspective, whether your relationships are supporting you or they're taking away from you.

As we start to grow as individuals, we tend to outgrow people in our lives who may not choose a path of personal growth. It's not a good or a bad thing. There's nothing wrong with them for not choosing that path. But if we keep trying to hold on to the past, and living in the past, it actually ends up holding us back.

We do not only ourselves a disservice, but also we do the people we're hanging out with a disservice. Part of getting out the junk is taking a look at your relationships and assessing whether they're serving you, and whether you're serving others in your relationships. We all hang on to people we've outgrown to kind of pull them along. The best way to help others is to let our light shine so we can be the example of what is possible.

Relationships Are Everything

I learned something really awesome in nutrition school. We learned a lot, obviously, about what you eat and how it affects you, but we also learned about something called Vitamin L: Vitamin Love.

We also learned about something called *Primary Food*. In this country, we talk a lot about "food-food" — stuff that we eat — but we don't really talk about the other stuff: the nonfood stuff, the stuff that really feeds us on a deep spiritual level.

In this case, one of those nonfood things that feeds us is our relationships. Relationships are our everything! And if you don't believe me, go and hang out with your three besties all in one day and then tell me if you have those same cravings for sugar, salt, or carbs like you usually do. I know I don't. But give me an overstressed day with little to no positive interaction and I'm looking in the cabinet for something to "fill me up" at 8:00 p.m., guaranteed.

T. Harv Eker talked about how the person you marry will make or break the level of success you will have in this life.

When I first heard him talking about that, I thought: *Well, that's interesting. What does he mean by that?*

The longer I've been married to a solid, fun-loving man who is willing to ebb and flow with me and the uncertainty of life, I really see what it's like when you're energetically in alignment with the person to whom you're closest. You don't necessarily have to be married to him or her. It could be the person you're living with, or you're in an intimate relationship with; it's that core relationship — when you're energetically aligned — life really takes off.

Have you heard people talk about a power couple?

When I heard that I just thought: *What the hell does that mean?*

Now I see that it's how the couple is in alignment:

- Their energy
- Their ideas
- Their beliefs
- Their goals

They align. There's nothing more powerful than two people, or a group of people, who have common thoughts and beliefs; it's a very powerful place to come from in life.

Imagine the opposite, living with someone or having people in your life who are not in alignment with your beliefs, your thoughts, and your way of being. You can see that there would be friction there. They wouldn't be supporting you in having your best life, your best health, your best everything.

Defining What Is Healthy for You

Remember "Know Thyself, Know Thy Worth"?

It's really important, especially as a highly sensitive woman, to figure out what is healthy for you. What works for someone else may not work for you.

1. Who are the people in your life with whom you can be your best self?

   By that I mean: If you're goofy like me and you like to drop f-bombs once in a while, who are the people who not only love it, but they get juiced up around you and you get juiced up around them?

   When you're with them, you're not in your head at all. You can just be yourself. These are the people you want to be spending your time with.

2. Who makes you feel energized?

   You know that person: The one you go out with and even though you get home at 2 a.m., you have more energy than before you left. That one!

3. Who makes you feel more radiant and confident by just being around them?

There are people I love and who love me, but after spending tons of time with them, I just don't feel my healthiest, most radiant, most unshakably confident self. So that's something else to consider. It doesn't mean you don't love these people. Find those around whom you feel your healthiest around and have your best thoughts. Choose them and do fun things with them.

When you're with people who support you in being your best, you feel like life just flows. Those are the people that you want to spend the majority of your time with.

Regarding family: There are probably members of your family somewhere whom you feel a little tension with, to put it mildly. You could try to avoid them altogether and skip family functions. But others in your family will want you to attend.

There are strategies to making it through this kind of event:

- Set up boundaries around how much time you spend in the person's presence.

- Promise yourself that you will not say anything to provoke them. (These people usually don't need any provoking.)

- Rather than add fuel to the fire, check your ego at the door.

- See if there's a lesson that you can learn that day by being in their presence and make a promise to yourself that you will not allow yourself to get rattled.

My biggest life lessons have come from people with whom I didn't naturally get along. Maybe it's the magic of mirroring.

Taking Inventory

While I love information and self-help books, it's what we *do* with the information that really helps us maximize our potential and grow to the next level. Here's a little action item that I would love for you to do. It's about taking inventory. It's about thinking about all the people you have in your life—even the ones whom maybe you don't spend all that much time with. It applies to everyone in your life.

Around whom do you feel you are your most confident self?

Around whom do you have your best, most creative ideas?

Who has a positive influence on your life?

Around whom do you feel like anything is possible?

Someone told me that I am the sum average of the five people I hang out with the most. That made me really look at who those five people are. Because if I'm the sum total, man, I better look at that.

Who are the ones you hang out with the most?

Choose to be with people who will help you and whom you help:

- To grow to the next level
- To be the best version of yourself

It's a great moment when you realize that by deliberately choosing the people with whom you spend your time, you really can be in control of where you're going in your life.

Action Item

If you like charts, go ahead and create a chart. You can list the five people you spend the most time with.

Include columns on your chart:

- How do they make you feel?
- Are you your best self around them?
- Do you have more energy after you interact?
- Do you have an impact on them that is positive?
- Does that impact come back to you and you feel good supporting them?

Then you can really concretely take a look at who these people are.

The next piece after inventory could be to start adding other people into that circle, almost like your wish list.

Who you would like to include in your circle of five?

Then you can start moving in that direction.

Have fun with this! It doesn't have to be something so heavy, wondering how are you going to tell so-and-so you don't want to hang out with them. It's nothing like that at all.

When I started doing this in my life, I just naturally got busier around the people who I felt didn't resonate with me. I prioritized other aspects of my life. It evolved naturally. I started hanging out with more people who were in alignment with me, my goals, and my beliefs. Keep it fun and light. It doesn't have to be confrontational.

As you start changing your thoughts about the people you want to hang out with, you will just naturally start to attract the people you want in your life. You just have to set an intention and then move in that direction.

DECLUTTERING YOUR MIND

When I started to understand that I really could control not only how I feel on any given day, but also what I wanted to see happen in my life, I saw the importance of decluttering the mind. I've watched clients do this as well and over time, they have attained the body, the career, and the life they really want. Simply said, they started to unleash themselves.

By that, I specifically mean becoming conscious of what I'm thinking about. If it doesn't align with where I want to head in my life, then I need to find ways — the way you weed a garden — to weed out those unhealthy thoughts.

When you start doing that consistently, and planting new seeds of thought, you start to manifest change in your life. I have seen it time and time again with my clients, my husband, and myself.

The Power of the Mind

The mind is *so* powerful. Don't just take it from me.

I'm sure you can think back to a time when you experienced something people would call a coincidence. A coincidence is when two incidents coincide; all of a sudden, you were thinking of someone and then they called. Or you were hoping, even obsessing, about seeing so-and-so today, and then you see them walking down the block when usually, you *never* see them.

How could that be?

What we think about, we create. It's easy to get stuck on thinking about things you don't want in your life — like for the body, a lot of women will talk about their flabby stomach or celulite-y thighs. Sometimes it's talk about what you don't want to have happen, what you're worried about.

Wherever you put your thoughts and your energy, you create more of it. In terms of the the body, my experience is that my upper half just gets in shape so much faster than my glutes and my hamstrings and my quads (meaning my butt and my thighs). When I started focusing on the positive areas of my body, the lower half started to get in shape so much quicker than it ever would have. It's because I was focusing on things that were working. Then I felt motivated to do whatever it took to get my entire body in shape. Those negative thoughts were no longer zapping my energy and cluttering my mind.

In order to get more of what you want in your life, try to lighten up those thoughts, and get yourself to focus on the positive aspects of your health or on your body or whatever you want to change. You have to stay in a feel-good, positive space.

When you start noticing the unsupportive thoughts that creep in all day, you are on the road to change. This is the biggest revelation for people: if you can see how you keep creating what you *don't* want, that will become what I call *social proof* of why the hell you want to start putting more focus on decluttering your mind.

When I work with clients, my job is to point out those habits of thought. Maybe you've been talking a lot about how you want better friends and people who really accept you for who you are, but you keep finding yourself in this circle of women who aren't as supportive and you aren't your best self around them.

I would say, "Let's just think about what kind of thoughts you're having these days."

Start to take inventory on your thoughts throughout the day.

Are you predominately thinking about what's wrong with your friends?

I would guess that you are. Once the shift occurs and you spend more of your day thinking about what you want instead of what you currently have in your life, the shift will start and more of what you want will come in!

The Power of Affirming What You Want

Mother Theresa was not only an amazing, authentic, beautiful human being, but she was also super smart about the connection between thoughts and reality.

She said, "I was once asked why I don't participate in anti-war demonstrations. I said that I will never do that, but as soon as you have a pro-peace rally, I'll be there."

At the time I heard this, I was much younger and I thought: *What the hell is the difference between anti-war and peace?*

But if you really take a look at it, and dissect it, an anti-war rally is focused on war. It's got the word in it. A pro-peace rally is focused on peace.

It's the same thing with people who say, "I really don't want to be fat or sick anymore,"

My response is: "Oh my gosh, let's just turn that around, and let's find the positive on that."

Because when the subconscious hears *fat and sick*, that's what you get more of — fat and sick.

Start turning it around and affirming what you want. My husband is a big advocate of this. I have never seen someone turn around a business or his life more than him. Honestly, I live with the man.

My husband affirms what he wants, day in and day out, with one of these really cool affirmations a really good successful friend of ours had given us:

Today is a great day, and I have the opportunity to show up as the best me ever.

I am an irresistible magnet with the absolute power to attract into my life everything that I desire.

I started saying that, and my husband has been saying it every day for about two years now. I've noticed since using that affirmation, the world starts to come around and gives you evidence that today really is a great day. Being consistent is the key. Make a commitment to affirm what you want by writing it down and allowing yourself to get really excited as you think about it coming to you.

Finding What Works for You

While everyone is in-tune to some degree, highly sensitive women are even more dialed in. So more than ever, there is no cookie-cutter method that will work for everyone. You need to find what works for you. My guess is you tend to not to go along with what works for the masses anyway, but consider this a good reminder.

Those who have kids know that no matter how many you have, every kid comes out so differently even if they are raised by the same parents and are treated the same way. They're all different. With that said, you need to find what works for you to declutter your mind. When you have moments of release, that means there is something in you that just opened up and we need to keep opening it up. It's not a moment of weakness as so many think. It's actually where your greatest power as a woman comes from — your emotions.

I'm going to give you some examples, because sometimes when my clients hear *declutter your mind* for the first time, they wonder what the hell I'm talking about.

Let's say you're in yoga class, and the tears start coming. Instead of trying to make them go away, I want you to have more of them. Really. Because when you have moments of release, whether it's a good cry or a good run, your endorphins kick in.

You might experience release during activities such as:

- Hot yoga (that was a really big game changer for me)
- Going for a long run

- Weight training
- Walking on the beach
- Hiking in a beautiful place

A dear friend who's a musician says his best ideas come to him when he's lifting weights. They just come to him.

So what does all this mean to you?

Simply that you need to find what works for you! I also find getting bodywork done is really good, particularly for those who want to tiptoe into this. Maybe you have never experienced what I'm talking about, but you want to be able to access the concept of processing emotions and get some old, negative thoughts out.

Bodywork and therapies can help to bring old issues to the surface to help you begin to process them. These include but are not limited to:

- Massage
- Reiki
- Acupuncture
- Emotional freedom technique (EFT)
- Neurolinguistic programming (NLP)

The best way to figure out what is next for you is to find people in the healing field with whom you resonate. You'll know when you meet them whether you do or do not. You'll feel comfortable in their presence. You'll want to come back again. Find those people, and then start working on yourself so that you can really start decluttering your mind and making space for all the good, new, positive thoughts that are just knocking on your door, trying to get in.

Who's on Your Team?

Just like it takes a village to raise a family, it takes a team to be successful. It takes a team to help get you where you want to go. Don't just take my word for it.

Once I learned that the number-one golfer in the world has a whole team of people helping him be at the top, it just made sense to me. Having a team of people helping out is what a smart, successful person has in their life. They're not weaker because of it, they actually know their worth.

I've been a coach for over a decade. I create nonjudgmental, supportive space to help people just be able to think about what they want. I know from experience that clearing out the clutter will help you to get to that next place in your life that maybe you thought you could never get to. If you haven't joined my community of empowered women yet, maybe now is the time. Go to my website at www.jenneddencoaching.com and see what I'm up to! I promise you won't regret it.

What will you find when you clear out the clutter?

- In your house
- In your relationships
- In your mind

When you clear all that out and do it consistently, your whole life changes for the best. Again, don't take my word for it. In fact don't take my word on anything I talk about. Try it for yourself and then you'll understand firsthand that what I'm talking about works. And that, my friend, is how real change happens: when you experience what I'm talking about and get excited to see more.

BRYANNA'S TESTMINONIAL

I have always had an addiction to sugar and Jenn's unique story as a recovering sugar-a-holic and her way of simplifying the complex really resonated with me.

I have never worked with a health coach before so I was excited to have someone in my corner helping me figure out how to manage my ultra-busy growing career, plus four kids, while attempting to get us all to eat a healthier diet. (Jenn knew from the start I was not going to cut anything out of my schedule.)

Working with Jenn has been amazing. She has this unassuming way of making you feel appreciated for what you're already doing and excited to make more changes. I catch myself feeling surprised by how easy it's been to make changes to my diet and lifestyle already.

I am definitely getting what I was hoping for and more from working with Jenn. I would, without a doubt, recommend her to anyone who thinks that their ultra-busy life does not allow them to fit in time for themselves and getting healthy!

~ Bryanna Royal
Founder, Virtual Powerhouse
www.virtualpowerhouse.com

CHAPTER
FIVE

Your Life Unleashed — Here's How-To

FIND YOUR FUN

Children are happy because they don't have a file in their minds called "All the Things That Could Go Wrong."
~ Marianne Williamson

I cannot stress enough the importance of having fun on your way to creating that life you always wanted. I wholeheartedly believe we were put on this earth to experience joy and peace and that life was meant to be enjoyed through the ups and downs.

So often we grow up believing that having an awesome life we wake up to every day is something just outside our grasp, that others are deserving, but somehow we are not.

We believe that if we only had the degree, the talent, the money, the parents who supported us more growing up, then we could have a life that juiced us up.

I'm here to shed some light on this false way of thinking that has up until now kept you stuck.

You too can create that awesome life, but first you have to learn a few secrets that I've picked up in my work over a decade with women.

Ever notice how much fun kids have doing pretty much anything?

According to psychologytoday.com, the average four-year-old laughs three hundred times a day.

The average forty-year-old?

Only four.

Why is that?

I say it's a learned behavior, and the buck stops with me.

As we get older, the natural tendency is for us to equate getting older with:

- Less fun
- Less energy
- Less laughter
- More work
- More bills
- More complications

It's just a natural inclination for people. Since I'm here to help you unleash yourself and get you that radiant energy and unshakable confidence, we must look at this thing called the *fun factor*. If you're not having fun along the way, you're more likely to end up quitting; not because you couldn't accomplish your goal, but because there wasn't enough fun sprinkled into your day.

Remembering What It's Like to Be a Kid

I equate fun with being a kid. I'm a mom of three kids; I see them having fun all the time, no matter if they're eating dinner or waiting for the bus. They are a great reminder that we're just meant to have fun on this Earth. Life shouldn't be a chore, it shouldn't be something difficult or a struggle. We're here to have fun.

Yes, I realize if you own a home or property, or run a business, or are caring for a sick parent, maybe it's not fun all the time. You need to handle your responsibilities. But then, make sure you add in fun somewhere else in your day or week. Waiting for that next big vacation is too far away.

Think about children and how they have fun: You can buy them expensive, fancy toys, and then you turn around and they're playing with a refrigerator box. They come up with the most creative ways to play with it. It's their top toy for the next two weeks. It's just so natural for them. Watching my kids reminds me that life is as fun as you make it. You can have fun with just about anything you can think up.

If you can get back in touch with the kid in you, that is where the magic happens. That is where you start to manifest things in your life that you've wanted.

For me, my goal for many years was getting in shape and getting a body I loved. I like to feel good, look good, and be strong so I can play with my kids and not tire quickly. I started taking classes and finding personal trainers. Then I started deciding to go for a run because it was fun, not because I thought I could grit my teeth and bear it for five more miles and then I would have that tight ass. It just doesn't work that way.

My experience working with women has shown me that most people model their lives on their parents' lives. Take a look; if your parents were all about fun, well then you could almost skip this chapter because my guess is you already know how to have fun. It's ingrained in you from when you were small.

If you grew up in a family like mine, where my grandfather worked on the ships day and night and taught through his actions what it was like to put in a good day's work, then fun wasn't exactly on the top of the list.

Guess what my mom learned from that?

And guess what my brothers and I learned?

Is that so bad?

Nope.

My entire family, including my cousins, uncles, and aunts are some of the most sincere, honest, hardworking, successful business owners I know.

Does that make them bad people?

Nope.

But for sure, my grandfather played a part in the work-hard aspect of their lives. It's the stop-and-smell-the-roses part of life that I watch us all struggle with. Ask any one of my first cousins if they ever sit down. It's literally a joke in the family.

Having Fun Frees the Mind to Do Its Thang

If you're a type-A person with drive and passion, you tend to go-go-go. When the tank is empty, you push yourself to the point of collapse. I find that this mentality of "just one more task" can wind you up like a coil. You are accomplishing a lot, but you are actually cutting yourself off from your creativity and joy. Then, only when you give yourself that treat or that alcoholic beverage are you able to unwind and have fun. This is a huge part of the work I do with clients when we are working to kick those cravings for the long term. A tired, mentally worn out woman will always crave sugar. Always.

Does any of this resonate with you?

Having fun:

- Frees your mind so you can get back in touch with your creative genius
- Helps reduce cortisol that zaps your energy, causes cravings, and keeps the weight on
- Helps you unleash your greatest self

I had been in business for about five years when I was ready to grow mine and reach more women. Back in the day, my mentor was amazing on so many levels. She had a beautiful family, she made big bucks with a biz she loved, and her network of friends and colleagues adored her. Not too shabby.

I said to her, "So what should I be doing? I'm stuck. I don't know what to do. That next big idea is not coming."

She said to me, "Go take a break for the next two weeks, have lots of sex with your husband, and then come back and tell me what creative ideas come."

You know what?

I did it. I allowed myself to just breath and have fun.

This was a life-changing exercise for me. Out of that break I created my signature 21-Day Reclaim Your Mojo Clean Eating Challenge. It just came to me effortlessly during a couple of workouts. So I will never forget that it's not just that it sounds good, but this shit actually works! It really helps you tap into who you are and what's next.

What Makes You Feel Good?

The purpose of this book is to read it, and take it in, go ahead and enjoy it, but you know I'm all about action. That's where people stumble: they read great books with the best of intentions. But at some point you have to put the book down and take action.

A client was just telling me today, "You know, Jenn, the difference between your coaching and these books by amazing authors who mean well is that with you, I'm taking action every week. You keep me accountable. I write lists of things I want to do and what has been getting in the way. Even after reading all those books, it wasn't until after working with you that I actually started to get my life moving in the direction that I've always dreamed of."

That client is a writer, a mom, and now she's a business owner too.

To take action, you need to find incentive. I want you to take a moment right now to write down what makes you feel good.

Once again, this all sounds great in theory, but to work, you have to write it down.

Action Item

So here's a quick writing activity to get you thinking. Write your responses to these questions:

- What do you consider fun?
- What's been getting in the way of you having more fun?
- What's one thing you can do RIGHT NOW to make room for more fun?

Get it out of the mind and onto paper. Really. This is just another great chapter that you've read, but if you stop at reading it, it's not going to move your life forward.

I'll give an example, because I know that always helps: What makes me feel good and what I find extremely fun in this moment is getting up and working out at 5:30, at least three days a week, sometimes four or five. It makes me feel good, and I feel like a kid; I'm up, no one else is out, I hear the birds, I drive my Jeep alone over to my workout place, and I'm singing songs, no one is there to pull me away from my thoughts and I feel free! I love that.

The other day, my kids and I decided we were going to goof off. We went out for lunch, ate some ice cream, did some people-watching, came home, and we took out our kiddie pool. It's blue with fish painted on the bottom, takes about fifteen minutes to fill, and has a plastic slide. We jumped in and laughed and had so much fun! We muddied up the yard and laughed some more.

I called that my *Have Fun, Do Whatever the Hell You Feel Like* day. Make time to do stuff like that; just get out of your head. Go do stuff that reminds you of what it was like to be a kid, because let me tell you, eating that butter pecan homemade ice cream with my kids was pure joy! We all need that.

If you haven't done it yet, make a list right now — set a timer if you want, five minutes — and figure out some things that you can incorporate into your everyday routine that make you feel freed up and bring out the kid in you.

This isn't difficult, and it shouldn't feel like a to-do on your to-do List. If it feels that way right now, don't do it right this second. Do it when it feels like it would be fun to do it. You've got to do the exercise when it feels like it would be fun. Don't force yourself.

STAY IN THE FLOW

First, get in the flow. Then stay in the flow. Some people don't know what the hell the flow is, or how to get in the flow, or how to stay in it. It's just some sort of concept from the book and movie, *The Secret*. It's about manifesting your dreams. It all sounded good, but I find people can't figure out how to do it.

Staying in the flow means taking this universal energy, the energy that's out there—whether you call it Allah, God, Buddha, or the spirit within you—and tapping into it. When you tap into the greater flow, your life can really work for you. What you really want will start to come to you more easily.

How Do You Know When You're in the Flow?

I was a self-help psycho. I was addicted to self-help books. I would read them and feel like I got it. I really understood.

Then nothing would happen, and I'd think: *Oh, next book! I got it!*

Then nothing would happen and I'd think: *What the hell?*

That act alone, saying, "What the hell? Nothing happened!" is exactly what would keep me *out* of the flow.

You see, the books never told you that. So I'm going to tell you now, that it's very simple.

You are in the flow when:

- You're feeling good.
- You're smiling.

- You have those good thoughts coming to you effortlessly and one good thought builds on another.
- You have tons of energy and life just seems to be "working."

This can happen especially when you're exercising. A lot of people become addicted to exercise, because they become addicted to feeling good. That is when you're in the flow, period! You can be in and out of the flow ten times in a day, depending on if you ate too much processed food that day, if you didn't sleep enough, or any one of the million other things that happen in life to pull you off your center.

To put it simply, you know you're in the flow when you're feeling good; you're having good-feeling thoughts. The minute you start thinking about what's not working, and you get cranky, or you start complaining, forget it, sistah. You are out of the flow.

Complaining is a big interruption to the flow. So this is the new, exciting reason to *never complain*, ever. I try so hard not to do it. I could count on one hand how many times I complain in a week these days. I won't do it, because I know it takes me out of the flow. It takes me out of that life energy. It's just not worth it, and I don't like doing it anyway, so I don't do it very often.

Fun is linked with good-feeling thoughts. Start taking note of how many times in a day you go in and out of feeling good, and if you're not feeling good most days, then I really want you to pay attention to the chapter where I talked about getting the junk out, and for sure, kicking the sugar. When clients do those two alone, it is *amazing* how suddenly they're able to get in the flow, stay in the flow, and then not feel like they have to work so hard to have good-feeling thoughts every day.

The first step is about becoming more conscious. Make it a daily practice to take note. It's not something that you'll get overnight. You might want to reread and reread and reread this chapter; in fact, I recommend that, for it to really cement in your brain. It's just not an overnight process. I've been working on myself for more than twenty years doing this work — more than twenty. That's a long time. You've just got to give it time and have patience. Think positive thoughts! You've got to think the positive ones, otherwise you're defeating what we're working on here.

Do Flow Activities

Imagine you're in a bookstore, reading all these great books.

You think: *I've got it!*

Then you go home and shit happens, and you think: *Wait a minute — in the bookstore I was feeling all motivated, and then I came home and it all went out the window. I can't access a thing I've learned. I even forgot half the shit I read!*

Here's the beauty: In order to have yourself start getting into the flow and stay in the flow, you need to do what I call *flow activities*. You need to do stuff every day that makes you more conscious of your old habits and naturally gets you into the flow.

For me, it's working out, hands down. I can be in the funkiest mood in the morning, and after working out about twenty minutes, it's like an on-off switch—bad mood, good mood. I'm feeling my best self again, which carries into the rest of the day.

You have to figure out what flow activities work for you. Over time you'll come to know what they are.

What makes you feel good?

One client I work with is in sales and she travels all week.

She said, "There's nothing that gets me in the flow, nothing."

Then like a light bulb switching on, she realized, "I really do love that the beach is right down the block from my house. I really love that my yard is so peaceful."

I said, "Well, hell, you don't travel every single day. How about those other days you just sit in your yard, or you just get up at 5:00 a.m. and walk on the beach before work?"

It doesn't have to be 5:00 a.m., by the way.

If you're thinking: *Hell to the no!* then fine.

Make it 6:00 p.m. I don't really care. Just find a time that works for you, and go do it.

For her, that's been really helpful. She goes to the beach. She says she feels very close to Spirit there and it's really been helping her.

I bring this up because at first, a flow activity might not be obvious. But give it time and it will come. You need to figure it out for your own sanity and to maximize your potential.

Here's how you will know what your flow activity is:

- It will make you feel good.
- It will feel effortless.
- It won't feel like work
- It will be something you really enjoy.

Hang Out With People Who Are Also in the Flow

This one speaks for itself. You're going to start doing the things outlined here, and then you're going to start feeling good. There will be times when you get a phone call from *that* person who simply sets you off and then, BAM! You're ripped out of the flow.

All of a sudden, you think:

What the fuck?

I can't believe what a crap-ass mood I'm in!

See, the thing is, that's reality. I'm all about keeping it real. That's life. And at the same time, remember from the last couple of chapters, you are the sum average of the five people you hang out with the most.

Naturally, if you're hanging out with low-energy people, you're going to find that you're naturally going to be pulled in that direction.

Low-energy people can be:

- Moody
- Complain a lot
- Highly critical of themselves and others
- Always talking about others
- Judgmental

They are not bad people, but if you're a highly sensitive woman, you will definitely be affected by people like this. If you're hanging out with them, you might find that all of a sudden you get cranky an hour after you leave their company, and you weren't cranky before. You just absorbed their low energy and cranky mood and didn't even realize it.

People are allowed to be who they are, without judgment. You get to choose who you spend a majority of your time with. Now you know this theory of being affected by the people you hang out with. Hang out with people in the flow, and you tend to stay in the flow.

I've seen this before with mastermind groups I've worked in and in beautiful women's circles. There's something really magical that goes on when you hang out with other people who are also feeling good: common thoughts, common beliefs, and common energy.

Hang out with those people. Go find them. Make a list and stay in the flow. It should just feel easy and natural. Remember to find the people that you can be your best self around.

Who are the ones with whom you can just let your hair down, you're laughing, and the time flies by?

Those are the people you want to hang out with. You want to hang out with them a lot.

DREAM BIG

Our deepest fear is not that we are inadequate. Our deepest fear is that we are powerful beyond measure. It is our light, not our darkness that most frightens us. We ask ourselves, "Who am I to be brilliant, gorgeous, talented, fabulous?" Actually, who are you not to be? You are a child of God. Your playing small does not serve the world. There is nothing enlightened about shrinking so that other people won't feel insecure around you. We are all meant to shine, as children do. We were born to make manifest the glory of God that is within us. It's not just in some of us; it's in everyone. And as we let our own light shine, we unconsciously give other

people permission to do the same. As we are liberated from our own fear, our presence automatically liberates others.
~ Marianne Williamson
A Return to Love: Reflections on the Principles of "A Course in Miracles"

I can totally relate to playing it small. When you really dream big, and you honor those thoughts in you that you really want to have manifest in this lifetime, you give others permission to do the same, which makes it so much bigger than you. It could be that dream to write your own book, change careers, move to a new city, get a divorce, start a family, or sell everything you own and buy an RV and travel the countryside.

I don't know what it is for you, but you know what that is for you, deep in your heart. If you can allow yourself to acknowledge that that is something you want, that is step one to pulling it into you and having it manifest.

Step one is just acknowledging, and just becoming aware.

I say dream big; my favorite line is, "Go big or go home!"

What's the point?

What's the point if it's not something that excites you, then don't write it down; we'll get to that after.

This part of the book is just about giving yourself permission to ask for what you want, and to just start dreaming. I find that life gets busier and busier. Adults tend to dream less and accept what is.

I say "Hell to the no!"

I am so not about accepting what is. I support you in not accepting what is either, and dreaming bigger.

Pick Goals That Matter

I'm going to call myself a goal-making whore right now — yes, *whore*. I have been making goals forever. I swear I came out of the womb making goals. It's just how my brain works. Now people pay me to help them set goals and reach them because I am so darn passionate about making this one life count.

But the thing no one ever really told me, even in all these self-help books, is to pick goals that really matter.

Pick the ones that scare you; the ones that make you think: *Hmm. Can I really do that?*

If you don't give yourself permission to pick goals that would really be life-changing, you won't generate enough energy to ever reach the goals. Seriously.

Passion = energy = more easily attracting what you want and getting it.

When I say life-changing goals, I'm referring to stuff you really want, such as:

- Getting that new business off the ground

- Getting a huge promotion that would change your financial picture
- Making a decision to start saying NO more than you say YES to free up your time and your life. Yup.

As an example, I'm thinking of picking my whole family up and moving cross-country because it's good to change things up and experience life. We're in the discussion phase of how and when, but it's up for discussion, which is a lot more than most people give themselves permission to do.

So do yourself a favor: allow yourself to dream, pick goals that matter, the ones that scare you. Then get the support to get them handled. I'm all for getting help, obviously; it's what I do, and I know it works.

Passion & Enthusiasm

+

Big Goals

+

Support and Accountability

=

Unleashing Yourself and
Getting What You Want

Life Is Short: Find Your Gratitude

We hear it all the time, like a cliché: *Life is short.*

You say to yourself: *Yeah, blah, blah, blah, blah. Let me just go on with my life.*

Well let me get real personal for a moment and share with you my near-death experience of living through "life is short."

My husband and I were married for four months, renting a house in Hicksville, New York. I was away on business and then I came home from being picked up at the airport by Joe to a house filled with gas.

Long story short, the house blew up about twenty minutes after we got there. I was in the house, looking for my two cats when my husband yelled at me to come outside and not breathe in the gas. Within minutes the pilot light in the basement went on and the house was a bomb. I was literally blown out of the house; thirty-five stitches on the left side of my face, and my husband was blown off the back deck. We were lucky to be alive.

After dealing with all the trauma associated with such an event, I remember coming away with the following:

- I was alive.

- I had stitches above and below my left eye, where the back door hit me, but my eye was unharmed so I knew there was something there that God still wanted me to see.

- Everything is replaceable except people and pets. (Everything we owned had burned, with the exception of my wedding album and one of our beloved cats.)

- *Holy shit! Life is really short, so I'd better do something with my life because I don't know what tomorrow will bring.*

I make it a point to have daily gratitude for being alive. So I live "life is short," from a really personal experience. I know lots of people have their own near-death experience. Everyone's got something. I recently learned one of my cousins saved his brother from drowning in the ocean as a kid. You hear stuff all the time, if you really take the time to listen.

Some people just blow that off and then move on; I took my near-death experience to heart. I found my calling, got certified, quit my job, and never looked back. I just ask you to find what it is for you. I say find your calling. Find your meaning. It doesn't have to be as extreme as mine, but life really is short.

Life goes quickly, so why not treat it as such?

If you can relate to having some sort of tragedy, great, but if you can't, that's fine too. Just find for you what it is that you can be grateful for. Gratitude is a really important piece.

Maybe you're wondering, "Well, Jenn, how do I dream big and stay in the flow and have fun and whatnot?"

I find having gratitude softens everything in life. It softens the cravings, it softens if you have anger, or stuff from other people around you that triggers you. I find daily gratitude calms oneself. You can extend it to even start thinking about what you want to do, or what you want to do next. Having gratitude is a really important part of having big dreams.

If you can't be grateful for what you currently have in our life, how do you expect to have more?

What's in Your Jar?

People refer to those things you want to accomplish before you die as a bucket list, but I don't like that term. Since I don't do things I don't like very often, I'm picking a new term.

What's in your jar?

You know, the one you created as a kid that you put shells in.

Didn't we all have one of those?

I did.

Sometimes it's overwhelming to think about your whole life and what's on this list of things you want to accomplish. So let's keep it simple. Let's empty the shells you put in your jar as a kid and replace them with written notes of all those dreams, goals, and ideas that you've yet to accomplish.

For a lot of women, they have so much on their plates already that breaking it down makes it easier to come up with ideas.

Let's use a quick mom example I find very common in my circle: Say you're home with your kids for the summer or your kids are older but you still spend time with them. Maybe spending time with your kids goes into your jar.

If it's too much for you to set goals for your whole life, then just break it down by seasons.

Women I work with say the jar helps them not regret that another summer went by when they didn't do x or didn't travel to see y.

Here are a couple of mine to help get your juices flowing:

- I want to take my whole family for at least a month or two and visit every state in the United States. That's just what I want to do. I want to get an RV, all five of us, and I just want to drive.

- I want to see my kids skydive. It's something I did that I thought was life changing, so if they want to put that in their jar, I'll leave it up to them. For me, skydiving was a life-changing experience.

- I really want to go on an African safari. I want to be there, in nature, with the animals.

- Writing this book to impact lives across the globe — for people who are looking for the answers and haven't found them yet.

Please make it fun! You'll be amazed by what will comes out of your mouth and onto the paper. Put it on paper, so you can have it written and then alter it as needed, but just do it when you're in a good mood.

Action Item

What do you want to experience within this current season, the next year, or before you die?

- Get a jar, a mug, or anything that you feel comfortable keeping around the house.

- Set a timer for ten minutes.

- Write down what comes to mind. It's up to you how far out you want to dream.

- Put each big goal in the jar. Every time you think up a new experience or goal that scares you, put it in the jar.

- As you accomplish each goal or experience, pull out that paper to make room for new ones. The last thing you want is clutter in your jar.

As you go through the highs and lows of your day, that jar will be your reminder of where you're headed. You will be constantly reminded of what you want, and that's how you'll be sure to make it happen.

I like to dream big so I always write down the big dreams.

MAIREAD'S TESTMONIAL

I first sought Jenn's support because I was having trouble getting my diet on track and nothing I had ever tried worked long term. We met at a networking event and after one conversation I knew I had to work with her.

If I could sum up how I feel about working with Jenn it would be that she uses her dynamic personality and ability to simplify the complex to get people real results. She really helped me articulate what I wanted from our work together in a way that felt easy and attainable.

I have also found in the few months I've been working with her that I no longer dwell on the negative side of life and what's not working.

That's been a huge step forward for me. When I was able to get my food choices cleaner while at the same time decluttering my mind and home, I really felt my life coming together in a way I had never felt before! Jenn has a knack for going deep, as much as we allow ourselves, which has had a profound effect on me. From a health standpoint I've lost inches and my clothes have never felt better.

My diabetes is under control and I feel like I'm in control of what is next for me! Thank you, Jenn. You are a gem.

~ Mairead Barrett

Conclusion

If I had to guess, I'd say reading books that give you tons of information and ideas makes you feel inspired and motivated. You may have made some changes in your life even before you finished this book. If that's the case, way to go!

But others of you reading this may be thinking: *Some of this stuff feels impossible to me.*

Let me teach you something a mentor told me years ago and it kinda just stuck.

He broke down that word, *impossible*, into I-M-POSSIBLE, and it just blew the roof off of the old belief: *I can't do this!*

I am telling you right now that YES YOU CAN! You're no different from me. I just consistently do the things I've talked about in this book. I've witnessed countless people experience real change in their lives by putting one foot in front of the other and making one small change at a time.

Now if you're feeling like you don't know where to start, I have a few suggestions:

1. Involve a friend. Encourage her to buy this book and go through the exercises with you. There

is nothing more powerful than women on a mission together.

2. Consider hiring someone who is living the life you want and learn from them. If that step feels like too much, then attend a few seminars or workshops in your new areas of interest. Take some sort of action in the direction of what you want.

What I don't want you to do is to sit there and say to yourself: *That was amazing! Man, that resonates! Man, I could see myself making some changes!* and then put the book down.

Take some sort of action within twenty-four hours of either having read something you enjoyed, or finishing a book. *Do* something. When you do something, what you do is you set energy in motion. What we're looking to do is get out whatever stagnation you have by just getting you moving. So do something. Do anything.

Life is a journey; there is no final destination. If you allow yourself to view it that way you don't mind the ups and downs, because it's all part of life.

You will actually start to *want* to bring on change instead of fearing it. All the stuff we're talking about in this book is about change. Having a new relationship with change will be really helpful in you implementing step by step, one by one, all of the recommendations I'm making.

I want to instill that and remind you of that today as you finish this book.

Life is a journey and it's up to you where you're headed and how brightly you want your light to shine on the trip.

Next Steps

Because I am a woman of action, I'd like to offer you a few next steps to get your wheels of change moving right along.

If you're not already a member of my Jenn Edden Coaching Community, I invite you to head over to www.jenneddencoaching.com and join us now. You will receive my latest updates, announcements, and fun tips and tools to keep unleashing yourself.

If reading this book has piqued your interest in what I do and how I do it and you'd like a strategy session, head on over to www.jenneddencoaching.com and click Contact Me and let's see what we can unleash together!

Since I'm a huge fan of gifts, I'd like, in typical Jenn fashion, to offer you a gift today just for purchasing this book and taking yourself on!

Yeah.

Head on over to www.womanunleashedgift.com and claim it today.

Lastly, if you know someone who could benefit from reading this book, I'm all about paying it forward. In fact, I've given away more copies of my favorite books to friends and clients than I can keep track of. It's just how I roll. I invite you to do the same.

About the Author

Jenn Edden is a certified health coach specializing in sugar addiction and empowerment coaching. She is also a mom, speaker, and biz coach for other entrepreneurs looking for clarity and confidence. As a recovering sugar-a-holic, Jenn supports women to take back their lives and health by making small tweaks to food and lifestyle choices while addressing how much mindset plays a role in long-term success.

Jenn Edden, CHHC
Sugar Cravings Expert and Empowerment Coach

www.JennEddenCoaching.com
www.linkedin.com/company/jenn-edden-coaching
www.facebook.com/jenn.edden.coaching/
twitter.com/JennEdden
www.instagram.com/jennedden/

Made in the USA
Columbia, SC
21 June 2021